Pregnancy

in His Presence

The Journal

Philippa-Jo C Dobson

ISBN: 1492108251

ISBN-13: 978-1492108252

Pregnancyinhispresence.com

twitter.com/prespregnancy

facebook.com/pregnancyinhispresence

Contents

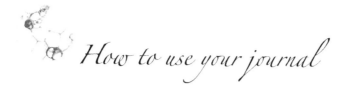

How to use your journal

This journal is broken down into each week of your pregnancy from week four to forty plus. Each trimester is indicated so you can easily find your way around.

Each week has a different theme with scriptures, thoughts, prayers, prompt questions and exercises around that theme.

The aim of this journal is to take you week by week, step by step, into a greater relationship with God. As you read each theme and meditate on the scriptures within that week you will grow into a greater understanding of God's love for you and His standard for pregnancy and birth. The journal will give you tools and tips on how to obtain that standard and what to do if you don't! The aim is not pain free labour, although that is a part of it. The aim is to help you in your journey of faith, in whatever you are believing for. I hope to take you on a journey from wherever your faith level is currently at, and lead you into a greater understanding of who He is and what it is possible for you to experience through Him. I hope that after you have given birth, whatever your experience, you will be able to look back and know that God was with you. My desire is that the experience you have will change you and teach you how to be a more dynamic believer and lover of God.

Each week you will be given a brief summary of how your baby is growing and some of the things your body may be doing. I encourage you to use the information to pray into and declare the right outcome over your unborn child. For instance *'Baby I speak to your heart, all four chambers form to the correct proportions. Begin to beat rhythmically. I declare that you will never need heart surgery or suffer from a heart attack or any heart malfunction. I speak strength over this little heart'.* If you are reading this before you conceive you can pray into the information given in week four prior to conception. If you're already at week four then begin to pray over your tiny baby. Pray that they are attached properly and grow correctly from the very beginning. Also, pray and declare over your own body for what it has to accomplish.

First Trimester

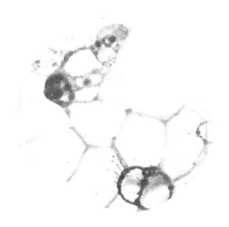

Weeks Four - Thirteen

Our family portrait!

A picture of me and Daddy, pre bump
This picture was taken:

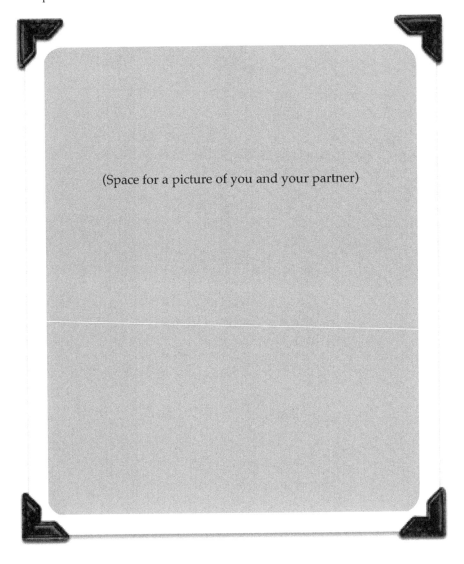

(Space for a picture of you and your partner)

Pre Pregnancy knowledge

Daddy's job: Civil engineer

Mummy's job: science teacher at Swain.

Combined income:

Daddy's age and date of birth: 30 years old
7/1/89

Mummy's age and date of birth: 30 years old
8/26/89

Siblings, names and ages: Ben Mitchell (32)
Kim Stauffer (33)

We always planned to have a family when: Although we went back and forth (or at least I did) we decided that we would want kids eventually.

This is my reflection on how I felt over the weeks before I realised I was pregnant with you: We tried for two months. Then I was starting to feel scared and conflicted if I could really handle being a mom. Well, God decided for me.

Week 4 - The moment of realisation

When I realised I was pregnant I was at: *on an overnight (3 day) camping + Kayaking trip in maryland with 6th graders.*

I took ...*2*... pregnancy tests because I: *wanted to be sure. I took them the next day when I got home.*

These are some of the emotions I felt when I found out I was pregnant:
Panicked, nervous, excited, Scared

This is how I feel about you, my tiny baby:
When I think of having an actual baby I feel flooded with love and anticipation.

> Psalm 139:13-18 *For you created my inmost being; you knit me together in my mother's womb. I praise you because I am fearfully and wonderfully made; your works are wonderful, I know that full well. My frame was not hidden from you when I was made in the secret place, when I was woven together in the depths of the earth. Your eyes saw my unformed body; all the days ordained for me were written in your book before one of them came to be. How precious to me are your thoughts, God! How vast is the sum of them! Were I to count them, they would outnumber the grains of sand. When I awake, I am still with you.*

When you think that God already knows your baby and is watching over him/her even now, how does that make you respond?: *It makes me feel at ease and reminds me that this is all about his plan, not mine and I shouldn't worry.*

When you think about becoming a mother what do you feel?: *I think it may be overwhelming at times, but I think I will be good at it.*

Are you ready for motherhood? *are you ever fully ready? But yes.*

On a scale of 1-10 how excited are you about:

- Being pregnant?   0......1......2......3...(4.)...5......6......7......8......9......10

- Giving birth?   0......1......2...(3.)...4......5......6......7......8......9......10

- Becoming a mother? 0......1......2......3......4......5......6......7......8...(9.)...10

> *1 John 5:4 For everyone born of God overcomes the world. This is the victory that has overcome the world, even our faith.*

How wonderful it would be to impact your child's life from such an early point. As you cultivate spending time with God and are immersed in His presence, your baby is also surrounded by a heavenly atmosphere. Even at this early stage, a life spent in His presence cannot help but be a transformational one after birth. Your baby can be born of God through the faith that you are now beginning to hold.

When you think about who your child will become what do you envision?
a confident, compassionate, caring, humorous child that puts others first. Independent, strong yet respectful to others.

How do you think you can cultivate an atmosphere of His presence in your pregnancy? *PRAY MORE. Listen to uplifting Christian music. Fill out this book. Read the bible. Go to church + lean on my Christian friends.*

Take the following verses and think on them, mulling them over in your mind, speaking them out loud over your body, and your baby. (*emphasis added to verses*).

> *(Luke 1.42) ..."Blessed am I among women, and blessed is the child I will bear!"*

> *(Philippians 1:6) Being confident of this, that he, who began a good work in me will carry it on to completion until the day of Christ Jesus.*

> *(Deuteronomy 28:11) The LORD will grant me abundant prosperity—in the fruit of my womb...*

> *(Malachi 3:11) "I will prevent pests from devouring your crops, and the vines in your fields will not drop their fruit before it is ripe," says the LORD Almighty.*

Comment on how these verses make you think and feel about the nine months before you:

That God has it under control. I need to put my faith in him that everything will be okay and how he intended it to be.

If you have any negative feelings or thoughts that arise concerning childbearing, give them to God even at this early stage. Re-read the above scriptures again and again, asking Holy Spirit to make the truths known truth to you. As you exchange your fears and any uneasy feelings with biblical truth, this truth will become your reality.

Prayer: Thank you so much for this beautiful baby that is growing inside me. I feel so...

Scared that my anxiety will hold me back from having a good experience. I need to trust that you will still see me through and I need not worry.

I am so thankful. God I am confident in your goodness and ...

Your never failing love and support. You take away my burdens and I need to just let you take them.

I know that you will see this baby through to delivery, help me to work in partnership with you. Transform my mind over the coming months. Let faith rise up inside of me. God, I give you my body, my soul, my spirit and my baby. I trust you because I know that you are good. Thank you for the journey I am on, I want to grow closer to you during this time. Knit this baby together in my womb and bless this baby.

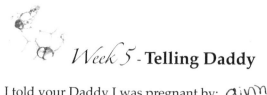

Week 5 - **Telling Daddy**

I told your Daddy I was pregnant by: giving him a new book to read. "We're ~~Parents!~~ Pregnant" A guide for Dads.

His reaction was: "Are you Serious?" Wow!. Thats awesome.

This is how I felt about his reaction: a little mellow, but that's who he is.

I plan to involve him in my pregnancy with you by: informing him on what to do for each step. This will be a partnership.

I have always thought of the father of my child behaving in the following way when I told him I was expecting: hmm... not sure, maybe a little more shocked?

God is your, and your baby's ultimate Father. Father God wants to be as involved with your pregnancy, childbirth, and child's life as much as you will allow Him to be.

> *Psalm 139:17-18 How precious to me are your thoughts God! How vast is the sum of them! Were I to count them, they would outnumber the grains of sand — when I awake, I am still with you.*

Right now, even at this early stage Father God has a plan for your baby. In Jeremiah 1:5 God says *"Before I formed you in the womb I knew you, before you were born I set you apart; I appointed you as a prophet to the nations."* He also has many thoughts concerning your baby. He was thinking of your baby before you were. God tells us that He already has plans for us, even before we are born. Jeremiah 29:11 says *"For I know the plans I have for you,"* declares the LORD, *"plans to prosper you and not to harm you, plans to give you hope and a future."*

Inquire of the Lord and find out what He has called your baby to accomplish in their life, even what their character is like. God knows every aspect of your child's future, He knows them even now. The dictionary definition for 'know' is: *'being familiar and acquainted with, being absolutely certain and sure about something. Being aware of, through observation, inquiry or information'.* So God is well acquainted with your baby, He has information about them and is observing them even now. God is omnipresent and widely regarded as outside the constraints of time, in which case He knows your child's life from beginning to end. If God is outside of time; He can observe your child at every stage of their life, pre birth, born, grown and even in old age, He really does know them better than we do!

> Proverbs 22:6 Train up a child in the way he should go, and when he is old he will not depart from it.

In which way should your child go? I suggest that this verse is not only implying that we train our children to love God and bring them up as godly men and women, but also that we should find the call of God on our child. All children should love God, but that will not look the same for each person. If God has graced your child with the gift of dance, has a plan for them to be a world class dancer and influence a generation with how they conduct themselves, then early ballet classes would work in tandem with this heavenly plan! I suggest that if our heavenly Father has a best plan for all of us then it would be useful for us to know what that plan and purpose is.

> Proverbs 25:2 It is the glory of God to conceal a matter; to search out a matter is the glory of kings.

God sometimes hides things for us to come and find, like a cosmic game of hide and seek that Father God wants to play with us. He wants to reveal everything in Heaven to us, if we are willing to go and look. If you want to know, then you can look and enquire as to what your child will be like and what is in store for them.

Spend time with God, find somewhere quiet, put on some music. 'Feel' His presence and listen to what He has to say about your unborn child. Use the space below to write down what He tells you:

"Blessings" by Laura Story is currently on the radio. I love + relate to this song because I feel like I've had a lot of trials that I've overcome + continue to work through and sometimes these painful moments in my life have made me who I am and have made me closer to God. "mercies in disguise".

So although I've been super anxious lately, this is just another trial I may have to go through until I find God's peace in this. I know I will love being a mom + I just have to lean on God in my moments of fear, because he has a perfect child in mind for me.

Note: Encourage your child's father to do the same thing, so that you can both begin to bond with your unborn child. It is good practice to buy a notebook and keep a 'prophetic journal' for the life of your child, it makes a great gift to present on their eighteenth birthday. Write in the notebook any time you pray for your child or when someone else gives you a word for them. I also have a "funny things, and milestones" notebook, in which I write all the quirky things my kids say and do. It's fun to look back on.

Father God wants to walk with you through this nine month period. It is a season of reliance on Him who is able to keep you from falling. Daddy God wants you to tell Him about how you feel throughout this journey and to cultivate a closeness that you have never had before. Use the space below and spend some time writing a letter to Father God. Tell him about how you feel about being pregnant, about being a mother. Include how you want to involve Him in this process of childbearing:

Dear Father God;

Please be near. Help me to feel your grace + comfort in times of anxiety and panick. Help me to enjoy this process and not allow my fear and anxiety to get in the way of what matters most. My beautiful child's heart is forming right now. My sweet baby is forming into a child that I'm going to love with my whole heart. Help me to focus on the amazing things happening now instead of letting the feelings of anxiety overcome me.

Growth: The heart beats for the first time, it's the size of a poppy seed and the first organ to start working. All four heart chambers are now functioning, and your baby's blood is now pumping. Most other organs begin to develop at this point, lungs start to form, along with the brain. The umbilical cord develops; Its job is to pump oxygen, remove waste, and supply the necessary nutrients to the baby while you are pregnant.

Extra reading: Do a word study of 'heart' in the bible. Find what God says about the heart and pray this over your child. Here's a few verses to start you off: 1 Samuel 12:24, Psalm 7:10, Psalm 27:3, Psalm 30:12, Proverbs 15:13, Proverbs 16:21, Malachi 4:6, Matthew 5:8, Romans 10:9

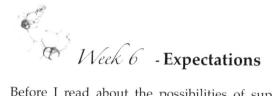

Week 6 - **Expectations**

Before I read about the possibilities of supernatural childbearing, these were my expectations for pregnancy and labour:

-
-
-
-

Through reading *Pregnancy in His Presence,* the one thing that has challenged me the most is:

I now recognise that these are the lies I believed about my pregnancy and childbirth. I have replaced these with the truth. Write in the columns below a list of lies or negative expectations followed by the corresponding truths you now know. If you are aware you are believing a lie but are not sure of the right truth, or if the truth you have found doesn't feel like it covers the lie, sit back and talk with God.

Lie	*Truth*
i.e.I believed labour would be painful	He took the curse from me

Ask God where you learnt the lie that:

.... (insert the lie you have, such as labour should be painful.) Then listen to what He reveals to you. You may, for example, get a snapshot of a conversation you had with a friend about their labour experience, or you may be reminded of a labour scene from a movie. You may not have realised that that conversation or clip had influenced you. You may find that you need to forgive that person or film for planting the lie. For example you could pray something like the following. "Jesus I choose to forgive my friend for scaring me into thinking that my experience could be the same as hers. I let her off for lowering your standard in my mind. I bless her with good pregnancies and births in the future. I forgive the movie director for portraying a funny but untrue picture of what labour should be like. I hand you the lie that I will have a horrific painful experience. Jesus what truth do you want to show me in exchange for this lie?" Following this example, take some time to converse with God and exchange several lies for truth, forgiving where you need to, even if it doesn't seem necessary. Forgiveness is a powerful tool, unforgiveness can hold us in bondage and stop us from reaching our full potential. Once you have dealt with the lie ask for His truth, if it doesn't feel sufficient keep asking or ask if you need to forgive anyone else.

After this exercise I now feel:

Prayer: Jesus I choose to align my expectations with the truth I now know, and I break the agreement with the enemy that pregnancy should be... *(List the lies you were believing.)* God thank you for showing me the truth, thank you that truth sets me free and I am no longer bound by my former expectations. I choose to stand on and believe the new truth that has been revealed to me. I declare over myself that my pregnancy will be... *(List the truths you now know.)* Holy Spirit I invite you to remind me of these truths anytime that I slip into my old way of thinking.

Take this list of truths this week and read them over yourself out loud everyday as many times as you can. Start now by repeating the list five times out loud. Note what happens to how you feel after the first few times of repeating the truths:

....

....

....
....
....

What we expect has a bearing on the outcome we receive. The gospel of Mark reminds us that we are to believe in our hearts, without doubting.

> Mark 11:22-24 *"Have faith in God," Jesus answered. "Truly I tell you, if anyone says to this mountain, 'Go, throw yourself into the sea,' and does not doubt in their heart but believes that what they say will happen, it will be done for them. Therefore I tell you, whatever you ask for in prayer, believe that you have received it, and it will be yours.*

However, it is important to remember that this principle applies to both positive and negative expectations. In Job it tells us that what we fear can come upon us. If we are expecting negative outcomes and lies, if we dread what is to come, then it can overtake us. Jeremiah 42:16 provides a solemn warning, *'then the sword you fear will overtake you there, and the famine you dread will follow you into Egypt, and there you will die.'* It is important therefore to cast out fear and realign our minds with the new truth we now have. We need to move away from dread into positive expectation.

> Hebrews 11:1 *Now faith is confidence in what we hope for and assurance about what we do not see.*

When we are confident in what we are expecting to happen, then we are in faith, and faith moves mountains! It takes twenty days for the mind to grab onto a new concept and for the old mindset to be broken. Over the next twenty days continue to read the list of truths and declare them over yourself.

So what are you expecting now? Write a brief 'vision statement' for what your expectations are for the remainder of your pregnancy and your labour.

From this day forth my pregnancy will be...

....
....
....

....
....
....
....
....
....
....
....
....
....
....
....
....
....
....
....
....
....
....
....
....
....
....
....

Growth: Your cervix and vagina have an increased blood supply, which causes a darkening in colour apparent by the sixth week. Elastic tissue increases to prepare for the stretching required during delivery.
The baby's arm and leg buds appear. The brain is growing well; over the course of the remaining months your baby's brain will develop over one hundred billion neurones. The lenses of the eyes appear. Nostrils are formed and the nerves running from the nose to the brain appear. Your baby's pancreas is now equipped with digestive enzymes, to take on processing the insulin and glucagons that the body needs to function.

Week 7 - Hearing God's plan

> *Jeremiah 29:11-13 "For I know the plans I have for you," declares the LORD, "plans to prosper you and not to harm you, plans to give you hope and a future. Then you will call on me and come and pray to me, and I will listen to you. You will seek me and find me when you seek me with all your heart."*

God not only knows about your baby, as we discovered in *Week 5 Telling Daddy*. He also knows all about your pregnancy and birth. God's standard for every pregnancy is health, but He knows you personally and there may be things that He reveals to you that can make your time easier. For example, words of wisdom about how your body works, timings of when to go on maternity leave, where to give birth and what kind of care you will need. God wants to be involved in this creative process of childbearing and He alone has all the information we need to walk through it confidently. He wants to guide us in every step.

> *Isaiah 30:21 Whether you turn to the right or to the left, your ears will hear a voice behind you, saying, "This is the way; walk in it."*

> *Psalm 32:8 I will instruct you and teach you in the way you should go; I will counsel you with my loving eye on you.*

For God to counsel us we need to be prepared to have a 'one on one' session with Him. The more time we spend with Him the more able He is to communicate with us. When you find time alone to be with Him, expect that you will hear His voice. His voice may be a small quiet voice like that of your inner monologue. You may also see pictures play in your imagination or get a general feeling or sense, you may even taste or smell something. As you spend time with God let Him use all of your spiritual senses to communicate with you.

Find a quiet place, maybe put on some music. Close your eyes. Focus your thoughts on Him. Feel all the exterior noise and all of the pressures from today quieten around and within you. Dial down everything else and find yourself in a place of peace that comes from His presence. Breathe in Holy Spirit and rest in His presence. Spend time listening to God. Let Him counsel you and give you information. Ask Him questions about the coming months such as: Where shall I give birth? Who shall I have present? How long will my labour be? Ask him what is on your heart; your concerns, your dreams. Talk with Him about what you want to happen, dream a little about what an ideal birth for you would look like, then ask questions that come to you from that. Write below what He says to you regarding your pregnancy and birth.

Note: *If you ask a question and you are confused with what you hear such as "Will my baby be born on time?" and your mind says "Yes, No, Yes, No." dial down in peace again. Command confusion to go. Ask another question such as "Will I need to be induced? If you continue to feel unrest use the next space to write in.*

God says my pregnancy will be...

....
....
....
....
....
....
....
....
....
....

Some things I heard I am unsure of, or feel negatively about:

....
....
....
....
....
....
....
....
....

Prayer: God I offer up to you these negative thoughts and ask you to give me peace in return. God help me to be sure and certain of the things that you have told me. I know that you have plans for my good and have nothing in store for me that would hurt me. I declare your goodness over my life and my baby.

Note: Sometimes God reveals to you the result of the current course you are on. For example He may know that your baby is laying sideways and this will make delivery difficult and may therefore result in a Caesarean. If when you pray you get a sense that you may need a C-section, there are many Christians who would take a deep breath and say, "Okay. This is what God has in store for me" because that is what they have heard Him say. However my stance on this is that God has given you the information to change your outcome. Jesus has given us all authority. If you know that He is good and He has plans to prosper you, then having a C-section is not the best way to prosper. (There is nothing wrong with having one if you need to, but obviously it was not the way that giving birth was designed to happen. Therefore to prosper we would at least have to follow the original design.) So, I think if you feel or hear a negative outcome, or if you have been told that you will have an experience that is less than the standard of Heaven and the Bible, then you have an opportunity. You can take the information that has been revealed to you and pray the opposite. If you have heard that you will have a caesarean, ask why, if you hear - because your baby is laying the wrong way, then you have the information you need. Speak to your baby and tell them to turn and to get into the correct position. Whatever you ask in faith will be done, if it doesn't happen the first time you pray, then pray again until you see it happen.

After praying for the things I am uneasy about, I heard the Lord say:

....

....

....

....

....

....

....

....

I now feel:

These are the scriptures that came to mind when listening to God:

When I saw the midwife for the first time she:

This is what I feel about my midwife:

We talked through the following issues:

These are some of the negative things I feel, heard or sensed:

This is what I intend to do about these negative things:

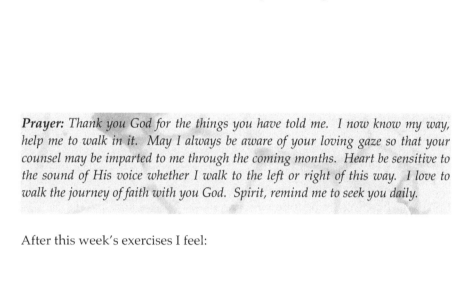

Prayer: *Thank you God for the things you have told me. I now know my way, help me to walk in it. May I always be aware of your loving gaze so that your counsel may be imparted to me through the coming months. Heart be sensitive to the sound of His voice whether I walk to the left or right of this way. I love to walk the journey of faith with you God. Spirit, remind me to seek you daily.*

After this week's exercises I feel:

This is how I intend to remember to seek Him daily:

Growth: Elbows form and they begin to bend and flex. Fingers start to develop. Feet start to appear with tiny notches for the toes. Ears eyes and nose start to appear. Intestines start to form in the umbilical cord, initially the intestines are formed outside your baby's body. Under the gums teeth begin to develop. Your baby begins to make its own blood in the liver, bone marrow and spleen.

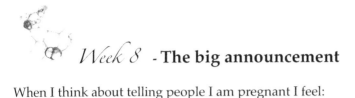 *Week 8* - **The big announcement**

When I think about telling people I am pregnant I feel:

I know I will get positive reactions from:

I may get negative reactions from:

I plan to tell people in the following way:

I have already told the following people and they reacted by:

I told them first because:

Telling people you are pregnant is a happy time. Most people will hug you and congratulate you, smiles all round. They are well meaning when they say things like, "Has morning sickness kicked in yet? No? You're lucky, but you still have a few weeks before your second trimester." And here you have a choice - what will you do in this situation?

I will answer in the following way:

These feelings rise up inside me when people say sentences like the above to me:

What are you announcing? You may not tell everybody exactly what you are believing for but what is the language that you are using regularly? Some things are so woven into our cultural norm that we don't think to question them. For example, to talk about and expect morning sickness and miscarriage as a standard part of pregnant life seems normal. Think about what you are saying. Proverbs 18:21 tells us *The tongue has the power of life and death, and those who love it will eat its fruit.* On one hand there is wisdom in not speaking too much, but also what we do say affects our outcome. Do not let yourself slip into idle normalities in your speech because it is easier. Our words hold the power of life and death. Set the agenda. The way you set the standard of speech is how people respond to it. If God is for you then it shouldn't matter who is against you.

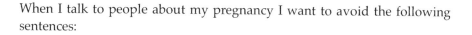

> *Luke 6:45 A good man brings good things out of the good stored up in his heart, and an evil man brings evil things out of the evil stored up in his heart. For the mouth speaks what the heart is full of.*

When people come out with the above phrases, what did you jot down that rises up on the inside of you? It is in this everyday occurrence that we find out what our hearts really believe. Then let's be intentional in what we want to portray.

When I talk to people about my pregnancy I want to avoid the following sentences:

-

-

-

When I talk to people about my pregnancy I want to remember:

-

-

-

Note: Remember to go back to Week 6 of your journal and re read the truth you now know.

> *Romans 12:2 Do not conform to the pattern of this world, but be transformed by the renewing of your mind. Then you will be able to test and approve what God's will is—his good, pleasing and perfect will.*

Having read this week's topic I know I have been conforming to the world's pattern in the following ways:

-

-

-

> *Psalm 16:8-9 I keep my eyes always on the LORD. With him at my right hand, I will not be shaken. Therefore my heart is glad and my tongue rejoices; my body also will rest secure.*

How shaken do I feel when people make negative comments about childbearing?

What does this tell you?

In what ways can you KEEP your eyes on the Lord this week so that your body can rest secure?

Prayer: God I thank you for the truth I have learnt about pregnancy. Continue to renew my mind so that my heart is full of truth. Help my thoughts to remain firmly in the realm of your Kingdom. May my speech not conform to that of the world. I choose your truth. When I hear negative comments Spirit remind me of the truth I know. Let a boldness rise up on the inside of me. Jesus set a guard around my heart that will stop any fiery darts from penetrating my mind. Jesus I choose to keep my eyes on you no matter how my announcement is received. I will not be shaken. I am glad that I am pregnant and glad that you have revealed to me that it need not be difficult or painful. Therefore help me to speak life over my body and my baby.

Go back to *Week 6, Expectations*, and read your vision statement over yourself five times. Be tenacious and fervent in your beliefs, not bull headed, but assured in what God has ordained for you, be unapologetic because it is your journey and it is personal to you.

Growth: Cartilage and bones begin to form. The tongue begins to develop. Intestines move out of the umbilical cord into the abdomen. The fingers and toes have appeared but are webbed and short. The vertebrae in the neck can bend and the trunk is able to straighten. At the end of this week your baby will have already completed 1/5th of the journey to birth. Baby's approximate length (crown to rump) is 0.61 inch (1.6cm) and weight is 0.04 ounce (1gm).

Extra reading: Do a word study of 'tongue.' See how many times it comes up in scripture then pray and declare each scripture over your child. Here are a few to get you started: 2 Samuel 23:2, Job 27:4, Psalm 12:3, Psalm 16:9, Psalm 34:13, Proverbs 12:18

✦

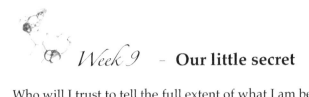

Week 9 - **Our little secret**

Who will I trust to tell the full extent of what I am believing for?:

This is how I know them:

These are the reasons I have chosen these people:

God, is there anyone who you think I should share my expectations with that I haven't thought of?

God, is there anyone who it would be easier for me in my journey of faith, to avoid telling?

> *Luke 2:19 But Mary treasured up all these things and pondered them in her heart.*

These are seven truths I am treasuring in my heart:
1:

2:

3:

4:

5:

6:

7:

Find a corresponding verse in scripture that shows you why that truth is real, write it below. Take one truth into your prayer closet each day, speak over yourself the relevant scripture, pray into it and see what additional revelation the Holy Spirit brings to mind. Ponder the words in each verse, mulling them over in your mind.

	Verse	*Revelation*
1		
2		
3		
4		
5		
6		
7		

Write below additional revelations God gave you on each verse as you prayed them through this week:

....
....
....
....
....

> *Matthew 6:5-8 "And when you pray, do not be like the hypocrites, for they love to pray standing in the synagogues and on the street corners to be seen by others. Truly I tell you, they have received their reward in full. But when you pray, go into your room, close the door and pray to your Father, who is unseen. Then your Father, who sees what is done in secret, will reward you. And when you pray, do not keep on babbling like pagans, for they think they will be heard because of their many words. Do not be like them, for your Father knows what you need before you ask him."*

Find somewhere you are most comfortable, laying in bed or the bath perhaps, get cosy, create a relaxing environment with candles if you wish.

Put on some quiet worship or 'soaking' music, Snuggle up, close your eyes and become aware of His presence. You can do this by hearing the lyrics of the music you are listening to, letting the words lead you into an understanding of who He is. You can take a passage from the Bible that depicts a heavenly scene, then let your imagination visualise that scene in your mind's eye, like the throne room of God. You can start by reading a passage of scripture like a psalm, then close your eyes and ponder its meaning. God has given us all five senses and we have mirrored senses in the spirit: we can see, hear, feel, taste and smell! You may be more of a sensory person and simply by closing your eyes and focusing your thoughts you will 'feel' or 'sense' a shift in the atmosphere around you, that is Holy Spirit, or the presence of God. Stay just relaxing in His presence, letting your thoughts reflect on whatever aspect of Himself God is revealing. Listen to what He has to say, at this time don't come to Him with a list of requests or a particular issue, just as it says in the verse above: *"For your Father knows what you need before you ask Him."* So rest in this quiet time and when you are done, write up what you experienced.

This is what my experience was like, or what the Lord revealed or said to me...

....
....
....
....
....
....
....
....
....
....
....
....
....
....
....
....
....
....
....
....

....
....
....
....
....
....
....
....
....
....
....
....
....
....
....
....
....
....

Prayer: Jesus thank you that you have revealed truth to me. Jesus I choose to take that truth this week. Make it known to me. I will ponder and think of your truth all week. I will keep in mind your promises until I know them to be true in my heart. Holy Spirit I invite you to speak to me regarding these truths this week, show me your word.

Growth: This week your heart pumps more blood around your body per beat and it will also beat slightly faster. Your blood volume expands twenty five to forty percent during pregnancy. Your baby has begun to move - while the movements are still too small for you to feel, your little one is wriggling. Most of their joints are formed now. Fingerprints are evident in the skin. Average size this week - length 0.9 inch (2.3cm), weight 0.07 ounce (2gm).

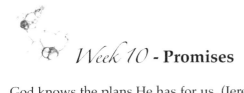

Week 10 - **Promises**

God knows the plans He has for us, (Jeremiah 29:11). We spent some time in *Week 5* finding out what those plans are, but how do we know these promises are going to be for fulfilled?

> *2 Corinthians 1:20-22 For no matter how many promises God has made, they are "Yes" in Christ. And so through him the "Amen" is spoken by us to the glory of God. Now it is God who makes both us and you stand firm in Christ. He anointed us, set His seal of ownership on us, and put His Spirit in our hearts as a deposit, guaranteeing what is to come.*

His Spirit is a guarantee. God is saying yes to us and has given us the ability to stand firm on what He has promised us. Sometimes our situation looks bleak and very far from what we have been promised. In Romans 4:18-21 the Bible tells us that Abraham was battling bleak circumstances but despite of them he still believed the promise. *'Against all hope, Abraham in hope believed and so became the father of many nations, just as it had been said to him, "So shall your offspring be." Without weakening in his faith, he faced the fact that his body was as good as dead—since he was about a hundred years old—and that Sarah's womb was also dead. Yet he did not waver through unbelief regarding the promise of God, but was strengthened in his faith and gave glory to God, being fully persuaded that God had power to do what He had promised."* Without His faith weakening Abraham faced the facts: in the natural his body was no longer fertile. However he did not allow the facts to override the truth of God's promise and therefore to lead him to a place of unbelief. He hoped and believed that God had power to do what He had promised.

List below what you know to be promises from God for you:

-

-

-

-

These are my natural circumstances:

In the following ways I will actively keep my spirit going after these promises:

-

-

-

> *Hebrews 6:12 We do not want you to become lazy, but to imitate those who through faith and patience inherit what has been promised.*

I know that I can be spiritually lazy in these areas:

So instead of being lazy I will:

Using the table below, list the most inspiring people of faith to you in the Bible:

Biblical Person's name	What they did that was 'patient in faith'	Why that inspires me

Now write a list of people around you, or those you know about that you can imitate:

Person's name	What they do/did that inspires me to imitate them	Where I heard about them

Growth: The most critical part of foetus development is complete. This is now a period of rapid growth. Your baby's head is about half the length it will be at birth, soon the rest of the body's growth will catch up, but this area is prepared to keep up with the rapid brain development. Eyelids are fused shut and irises begin to develop. The arms and legs begin to purposefully move. Around this week, your baby's placenta begins to function. Your baby will be about 1.22 inch long (3.1cm) and weigh 0.14 ounce (4gm) at the end of this week.

✦

Week 11 - **Health not sickness**

> *Isaiah 53:4 Surely He took up our pain and bore our suffering.*

> *Galatians 3:13 Christ redeemed us from the curse of the law by becoming a curse for us, for it is written: "Cursed is everyone who is hung on a pole."*

> *Romans 6:4-5 We were therefore buried with Him through baptism into death in order that, just as Christ was raised from the dead through the glory of the Father, we too may live a new life. For if we have been united with Him in a death like His, we will certainly also be united with Him in a resurrection like His.*

> *Romans 8:11 And if the Spirit of Him who raised Jesus from the dead is living in you, He who raised Christ from the dead will also give life to your mortal bodies because of His Spirit who lives in you.*

So far in my body I have been feeling:

List below the ways that you need to see health manifest in you or your baby's body:

-

-

-

Spend a moment and ask God if there is anything that you need to do in order to receive your healing more completely:

Think for a moment on the words you are saying about your feelings of sickness or pain. Does what you say reflect what you are believing? Or are you speaking death rather than life over your body?

In your own words, using the verses from this week and any others you find, write out below the truth about health and healing:

-

-

-

In what practical ways are you dealing with sickness?

What's the funniest remedy suggestion from friends and family you have heard?:

Write down practical things you need help with:

Who do you have that you can ask to help you in these areas?

Are there any time commitments or lifestyle areas that need adjusting to help you feel more healthy and restful?

Do you intend to change anything?

When do you intend to change these things?

.... (Write down the deadline date for changing these things in your calendar and hold yourself to it! Call a friend so they can help hold you to it too!)

In what spiritual ways are you dealing with sickness:

If we are seated in heavenly places (Ephesians 2:6) what is our heavenly perspective on sickness? The verse from Romans this week says, "*we will certainly also be united with Him in a resurrection like His.*" Ponder a moment then list below what it looks like to be united with Him in His resurrection life:

-

-

-

-

This week choose to kick out sickness. Write up three ways you intend to do this:

1:

2:

3:

Prayer: Spirit just as you gave life to Jesus, give life to my body. Body I speak to you and tell you to come in line with the new covenant, a healthy body. Body be healthy and made whole. Devil I take authority over you, and tell you to get under my feet, you have no power over me. I break every assignment from the enemy over my life and my baby. I walk free from the curse. Jesus I give you all my pain and suffering, thank you that you took it from me on the cross. I now stand in the good of the work you did there.

Think for a moment and then list the people you can turn to for personal prayer in the area of healing if you need it:

....

....

....

Also identify people that can commit to pray for you for the next six months to cover you in blessing for health, wellness of soul and a smooth pregnancy and labour. Write below who you have chosen:

1:

2:

3:

Write a list of your current prayer points and give a copy to your prayer partners:

-

-

-

Have them declare the following over you, plus anything else that the Spirit reveals to them as they lay hands on you: **"I speak to your body and tell you to be at peace. Body, soul and spirit come into unity with one another and be at rest. I speak supernatural grace over you and your baby. Holy Spirit I ask you to brush off anything from my friend that hinders her healing, we break every assignment over her and this baby and break any negative words that have been spoken over her. I extend blessing instead of curse. I agree with her and declare a healthy season. I speak to any sickness and tell you to leave in the name of Jesus. I release wholeness and resurrection power over every area of weakness in her body. Holy spirit I invite you, and the angels, to come and dwell in her home, and cover her with joy and gladness. Amen.**

Growth: Nearly all structures and organs are formed and beginning to function. Your baby is now medically called a foetus rather than an embryo because it appears more human. Foetus is Latin for 'young one' or 'offspring.' Fingers and toes have separated. Hair and nails begin to grow. The muscles in the intestinal walls begin to practice contractions that digest food. Your baby is about 1.61 inches (4.1 cm) long and weighs 0.25 ounce (7gm).

◆

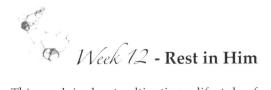 *Week 12* - **Rest in Him**

This week is about cultivating a lifestyle of resting in His everlasting arms. God wants us to draw away with Him and have individual times with Him without other distractions. No matter what your outward circumstances and life pressures are, find time in all you do to 'feel' the peace and rest of God. God wants you to feel His rest at all times, even when you are busy. Resting in Him is not about doing nothing, although sometimes that's what we need; it is being, in the midst of our busy-ness, at peace within ourselves. This week begin to develop a lifestyle of dwelling with Him.

> *Psalm 91:1-2 Whoever dwells in the shelter of the Most High will rest in the shadow of the Almighty. I will say of the LORD, "He is my refuge and my fortress, my God, in whom I trust."*

Everything in the Christian life needs to come from a place of rest; we rest when we trust someone. We trust Him when we know Him and we know Him because we spend time with Him. So it is from dwelling with Him that we find rest. We don't have to work for anything because Jesus made a way for us, He has blessed us without us deserving it.

> *Proverbs 10:22 The blessing of the LORD brings wealth, without painful toil for it.*

In my life recently I have been feeling stress/no stress because:

Write below three ways you can maintain the rest of God this week:

1:

2:

3:

These areas of my life are the most busy or stressful times or moments:

Have a think about these busy times and ponder how you would find or maintain the rest and peace of God in the midst of the busy-ness and stress:

I usually find it relaxing to:

This is what I am planning to do to relax this week:

I intend to spend the following amount of time having alone segments with God this week:

I usually encounter God best when I:

Do a Bible study on the word, 'rest' or 'peace' and write below seven verses that stick out to you:

1.

2.

3.

4.

5.

6.

7.

How do you intend to implement these verses into your life from now on?

Take a verse a day this week and ponder on it. Let Holy Spirit reveal further revelation of it to you and note what He says below:

....
....
....

Spend some time with God and ask Him the following questions...

Jesus why do I find it hard to maintain rest?

Jesus do I have a 'works' mentality?

Spend a moment and repent for any areas where you are not receiving grace.

Where did I learn this lie that I need to work to achieve?

Hand God the lie and forgive anyone who comes to mind as the teacher of this lie.

Jesus show me your truth:

....
....
....
....
....

....
....
....
....
....
....
....
....
....

Is there anything else that keeps me from resting or receiving peace?

Am I believing any other lies about rest and grace?

....
....
....
....

Prayer: God I choose to rest in you. I know that I do not need to work for grace and I freely receive it now as you freely give it. I choose to include you in my everyday life. I choose to set aside time to be with you alone. Spirit I give you permission to interrupt me this week, make me aware that you never leave me. Show me how I can develop a lifestyle of rest in really practical ways.

Growth: Vocal cords begin to form. Ears and eyes shift to their right position. Intestines move further into your child's body. The liver begins to function - it's responsible for cleansing the blood, storing nutrients and providing needed chemicals. The pancreas begins to produce insulin. Average length: 2.13 inches (5.4cm) and weight: 0.49 ounce (14gm).

 *Week 14* - **The Scan**

Baby, these people were at your first scan:

When I first saw you I:

During the scan you were:

Now I have reached the end of the first trimester I feel:

From your hospital notes write up all the scan measurements below:

> Jeremiah 1:5 *"Before I formed you in the womb I knew you, before you were born I set you apart; I appointed you as a prophet to the nations."*

Before we conceived our daughter, God told us she would be, 'strong in the spirit but also strong in the flesh!' This has helped me know how to be a mother to her now that she is here. You will have already written down some things God has told you about your child in *Week 5, Telling Daddy*. Now, spend some further time with God and ask Him again to speak to you about your child. Ask Him what plans He has for their life. Ask Him what their character will be like. And what gifting He has given them. Even though you have just had a small glimpse of your child through the scan, God has known them since before the beginning of time. He already has a destiny in store for them. Write below what He tells you. *(If the baby's Daddy is willing to do this too it is the perfect way to help them bond further, men often find it harder to bond as they are not experiencing the same bodily changes that your are).*

This is what God said about my child:

....
....
....
....

It was/was not what I was expecting because:

Hearing this from God has made me feel:

Knowing this makes me think about parenting in the following way:

I plan on preparing myself for a child like this by:

Having a child with this calling and destiny I need to:

Do some research into different personality types. You will be able to find online tests to discover your own personality type. Make a guess using the information you have been given by God to estimate which personality type your child will be.

My personality type is:

I found this interesting because:

I think my child's personality type will be the following because:

(*Note: the online tests usually list well known people throughout history with a particular personality once you have finished the test.*) Looking at famous people with the same personality type as your child, how do you feel about becoming their mother?

Having read up on personality types, how has it made you view yourself differently as a parent?

Another common test you can find is 'The love languages.' Each of us have five ways we receive love from others; through acts of service, physical touch, words of affirmation, quality time and through gifts. Picture each of these methods by which we receive love as petrol tanks that need topping up. Every time someone expresses love in one of the five ways that particular tank is filled. We all have a primary way that we feel loved the most and this is the tank that runs down the fastest. (You can read into this topic further in "The Five Love Languages For Children, by Gary Chapman and Ross Campbell[1]) Sit and think for a moment about which way you feel loved the most, you will have a primary love language usually followed by a very close second. (*You can usually find these types of tests online for free*).

My love languages in order of priority are:

1.

2.

3.

4.

5.

Your baby will also have a primary way in which they will experience your love, it will probably change as they grow. Take a few moments and think about what loving your baby will look if they experience and receive love with a different primary love language to you. Note how you see that working:

....
....
....
....
....
....
....
....
....
....

Prayer: God help me to be the perfect mother to this anointed child. Help me to identify the giftings in them early on, and give me the strength to nurture them. I know you have chosen me to be their mother. Help me and guide me. Give me strength and grace to love and discipline them appropriately for their particular personality. Jesus renew my mind to parent my child in the way that will make them the best adult they can be. Let me react to them with this in mind, help me not to default to how I was parented or how I would naturally parent.

Growth: Your infant is about 2.91 inches (7.4cm) and weighs around 0.81 ounce (23gm). Baby begins to practice inhaling and exhaling movements. Eyes and ears continue to move and develop. Baby's neck is getting longer, and the chin no longer is resting on its chest. The hands are becoming more functional.

First portrait!

Date:
Time:
Hospital:

(Space to stick scan picture)

Second Trimester

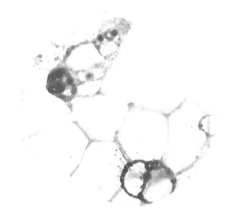

Weeks Fourteen - Twenty Seven

Picture of Bump!

Around the largest part of my belly I measure:

When I see this picture I feel:

People are now making the following comments:

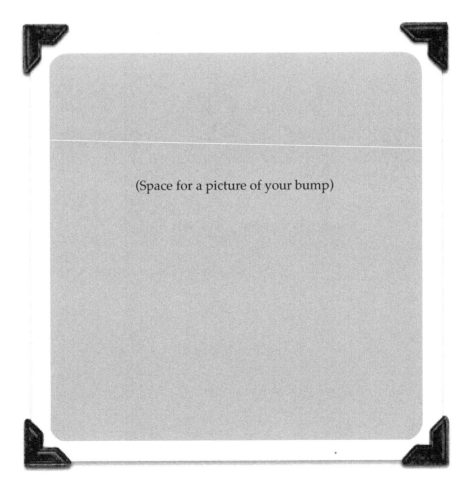

(Space for a picture of your bump)

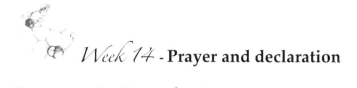

Week 14 - **Prayer and declaration**

Prayer is simply talking with and to God and letting Him talk to you. This week try and increase the amount of time you set aside to do this by a half. Don't just focus on devotional times but become aware of His presence all day, perhaps whilst you are driving or washing up. Connect with Him more often this week. Intentionally turn your attention and affection towards Him in your thoughts.

I usually spend the following amount of hours a week in devotional prayer:

This week I intend to spend:

I usually spend the following percentage of my day conscious of God and His presence:

This week I intend to remind myself that He is always with me by:

(tick as appropriate)

Putting up notes

Playing worship music

Setting alarms

Other, *(specify)* ...

I usually find it quite easy/hard to spend devotional time with God because:

Find someone you trust and respect to help you work through ways you can meet with God better than you do now. Speak to different people to see what they do to meet with God and write these below:

Suggestion	I would/would not find this helpful	Because

Close your eyes and wait for God's presence. You may get a sense that He is there with you. Picture one of the Godhead in your mind's eye.

Do you see Father God, Jesus, or Holy Spirit?

Where do you see them, what are they doing?

Are they close or far from you?

If they are far away see what happens when you take a step towards them:

Is there anything in the way for you to reach them?

If so, ask another of the Godhead that you generally connect with the most; "what do I need to remove this barrier?"

It may be that God brings to mind someone that you need to forgive. Sometimes we separate ourselves from God because we believe certain lies about Him, such as 'God is too scary to approach' or 'I am not good enough to be with Him.' Ask God what lie you are believing, and ask where you learnt that lie, forgive who comes to mind. Repent for believing the lie then ask God for the truth in exchange for the lie you give Him. For example, if our natural father was a distant disciplinarian type, then we will often think of Father God as distant to us and will hold the view that He wants to punish us. We can see in the Bible the truth that Father God has poured all His anger for sin out on Jesus at the cross so you can know the truth that He does not want to punish you. As you renounce the lie that God wants to punish you, ask Him for the truth, you may hear a verse about God punishing Jesus instead of us. You then can approach Him because you see that He is safe to approach. You can ask if it is safe to take the wall down and if you hear a 'yes' then ask God to remove the barrier. As it falls or disappears walk towards the member of the trinity that was behind it and be with them.

> *John 16:24 Until now you have not asked for anything in my name. Ask and you will receive, and your joy will be complete.*

During the times that you spend devotionally with God set aside some time to come to God with the things that you need to see change.

These are the items on my prayer list:

1:

2:

3:

4:

5:

6:

7:

Take one item every day this week and receptively pray them into being over the course of the day. Every time you have a spare twenty seconds, pray into them. Our words carry power, our prayers therefore can change the outcome of our current trajectory. *Proverbs 18:21 "Death and life are in the power of the tongue."* You are a son of God and you have kingly blood. A King speaks and it is done - so it is with you. Say to the mountain move and it will. *Matthew 21:21-22 Jesus replied, "Truly I tell you, if you have faith and do not doubt, not only can you do what was done to the fig tree, but also you can say to this mountain, 'Go, throw yourself into the sea,' and it will be done. If you believe, you will receive whatever you ask for in prayer."*

Write below a list of things that you can declare into being over your circumstances for yourself, and your baby: *(Take these declarations and speak them out each day this week while you do something else like the washing up)*. It's a declaration of faith, speaking things that are not, as though they were *(Romans 4:17)*.

1:

2:

3:

4:

Pick one of the truths from the list above and read it out loud now.

On a scale of one to ten how much do you believe it?...................

Repeat the truth you just read ten times, or using a stopwatch for one minute, either looking in a mirror or whilst holding someone else's gaze.

Having done this, how much do you believe it now on a scale of one to ten?..................

Note how you feel having done this exercise:

....
....
....
....
....
....
....
....
....
....
....
....

Prayer: God help me to spend more time with you and become more aware of you. Spirit rise up inside of me and intercede on my behalf. God may I become a person of prayer and of fellowship with you. God I choose to make time for us. Help me to understand the full meaning of being your son, a coheir with Christ. Help me to understand my authority.

Growth: The thyroid gland has matured and your baby begins producing hormones. In boys, the prostate gland develops. In girls, the ovaries move from the abdomen to the pelvis. Your child's bones are getting harder. Baby is able to swallow and urinate. Your baby is 3.42 inches (8.7cm) long and weighs about 1.52 ounces (43 gm) - approximately the weight of a letter!

Week 15 - Confession and meditation

To me, the word meditation often brings to mind an image of a new age style person humming! But meditation is God's idea. Everybody meditates. People give their thoughts and time to something but often it is to the wrong thing, on the wrong person, or with the wrong focus. One of the Hebrew words for "meditate[2]" literally means to murmur and implies the "moving of the lips, to mumble". Another word[3] means to converse with yourself. It is your inner monologue, the way you speak to yourself about things going on in your life. Meditation is not 'positive thinking' or encouragement. It's about faith. It is not about us, but about Him. New age meditation is about emptying your mind, but we are to set our thoughts on things above and realign our focus. Your meditation should be about the Lord. Think of what He has promised, what He has done. Think of His love, His power, His purpose and His word. As you do, you are lifted out of heavy thoughts about your circumstances; your cares are cast on Him. You begin to renew your mind and are confident that He cares about your life and situations. Scripture is the perfect place to start. Pick a few scriptures that either stand out to you or that you really want to get 'in' you. By now you should have read a lot of scripture regarding pregnancy and, hopefully, already have some of them stuck up around your home. Make sure you are reading them often. If not, or if you want some more, take some time to read the word this week and make your own scripture list.

These are the scriptures that I am mainly concentrating on:

-

-

-

-

-

These stood out to me because:

I usually read these scriptures this many times a week:

This week I will read them:

I plan on having them where I can see them in/on:

I choose to 'mumble' out these scriptures this week while I am:

Choose three or four verses and, out loud in a mirror confess them over yourself five times each day this week. Note how that makes you feel and think:

....
....
....
....

I usually read the Bible this many times a week:

This week I will set aside this amount of time to read it: *(Hearing The Word through audio Bibles, worship music and sermons are also a great additional way to immerse yourself in God's presence).*

Feed yourself this week with The Word. *Deuteronomy 8:3 He humbled you, causing you to hunger and then feeding you with manna, which neither you nor your ancestors had known, to teach you that man does not live on bread alone but on every word that comes from the mouth of the LORD.* The Word is our plumb line, if we know it we will grow straight. *Psalm 1:1-3 Blessed is the one who does not walk in step with the wicked or stand in the way that sinners take or sit in the company of mockers, but whose delight is in the law of the LORD, and who meditates on His law day and night. That person is like a tree planted by streams of water, which yields its fruit in season and whose leaf does not wither— whatever they do prospers.* When we happily make reading The Word a lifestyle we are like a tree planted by water; healthy and prospering.

Reflect how the above verses make you feel:

....

....

Growth: From this week on you may feel fluttering as your baby moves, but most women often don't feel any movement until the twentieth week. Baby can also grasp, squint, frown, grimace and maybe even suck its thumb! The three tiny bones in his middle ear have begun to harden. Your baby's brain hasn't developed fully yet so won't be able to understand what you say, but the hearing capacity is in the process of developing. (Although I believe the power of what you declare over them impacts their spirit). Fingernails and toenails are growing. Eyebrows are beginning to grow and even the hair on their head is sprouting. It will probably change colour and texture after birth. Your baby is now 3.98 inches (10.1cm) long and may weigh 2.47 ounces (70gm).

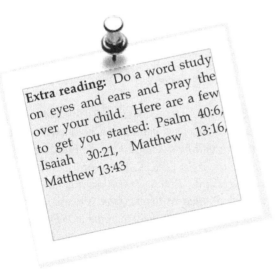

Extra reading: Do a word study on eyes and ears and pray the over your child. Here are a few to get you started: Psalm 40:6, Isaiah 30:21, Matthew 13:16, Matthew 13:43

Week 16 - **Eating right**

> *Psalm 34:8 Taste and see that the LORD is good; blessed is the one who takes refuge in him.*

> *Psalm 119:103 How sweet are your words to my taste, sweeter than honey to my mouth!*

We have talked about how we are not to live by food alone, but to make the Bible our source of life, *(Luke 4:4).* To eat from Him - the bread of life - and to go to Him and drink living water. Spending time with Him and reading His word are ways to feed our spirits. But what of our natural bodies?

My favourite food is:

Since being pregnant I have been craving:

I usually get this food by:

I usually exercise by:

Now I am pregnant I exercise by:

I have noticed the following changes in my habits and in my body:

God is a God of our whole being. Not only do we have a responsibility to edify our spirits and to keep our souls pure, but we are also responsible for looking after our physical bodies. What we put into our bodies is just as important as feeding our spirits and souls. 1 Thessalonians 5:23 says *"May God Himself, the God of peace, sanctify you through and through. May your whole spirit, soul and body be kept blameless at the coming of our Lord Jesus Christ."*

In what ways could you become less blameless in how you treat your body?

> *Exodus 23:25-26 Worship the LORD your God, and His blessing will be on your food and water. I will take away sickness from among you, and none will miscarry or be barren in your land. I will give you a full life span.*

As we choose to worship God and submit our spirits and souls to Him, He promises that He will also help us look after our bodies. He blesses what we eat. In our current day we are bombarded by advertisements for products that give us an easier and quicker lifestyle. Many of these adverts are for food, both healthy and otherwise!

Write a list of your top five favourite snacks or meals:

1:

2:

3:

4:

5:

How often do you have these foods a week?

In your opinion on a scale of one to ten, how healthy are these snacks and meals:

> *Colossians 2:20-21 Since you died with Christ to the elemental spiritual forces of this world, why, as though you still belonged to the world, do you submit to its rules: "Do not handle! Do not taste! Do not touch!"?*

> *1 Corinthians 10:31 So whether you eat or drink or whatever you do, do it all for the glory of God.*

The Bible is clear that everything under the sun is available to us to eat. However some things are not always helpful to us. *1 Corinthians 10:23 "I have the right to do anything," you say—but not everything is beneficial. "I have the right to do anything"—but not everything is constructive.*

In your mind visualise your dining table laid out with all the snacks, drinks and meals you have eaten this week (Be honest with yourself!) Now imagine Jesus walking in and putting His arm around you, you look together at what you have been feeding yourself on. (You can also do this exercise visualising how you have fed your spirit and soul. Imagine all the times you have read the Bible, prayed and worshiped in correlation to how much you have fed yourself with other entertainment, chores and daily responsibilities).

Looking at this mental image how do you feel?:

....

....

....

Are there habits or things you need to change for the benefit of your body and the life of your baby?
If so, what?:

....

....

....

How will you go about implementing these changes?

Ask yourself:

Am I eating the correct portion sizes?

Am I over or under eating?

Does the table look balanced?

Write below three ways you can be more healthy during your pregnancy:
1:

2:

3:

Spend time seeking God for wisdom as to what additional supplements, healthy food and lifestyle changes you can make in order to make your body work for you more efficiently.
Ask Jesus about the mental image of the full table, "what do you think of this table?"

....
....
....
....
....

Prayer: God I offer you my body as a living sacrifice. May I be holy and pleasing to you in my soul, spirit and body. Help me to address any area where I need to make changes. Highlight to me the things that I do that are not beneficial to me. I am sorry for not treating my body as your temple and I ask your forgiveness. From now on I decide to make what I do and eat all for your glory. Help me to overcome my stomach's desires and break the control that food has over me. God, thank you for making all things for me, help me to be wise in what, when, how and how much I eat. I choose to break away from what the world portrays as normal and instead seek your council. You know me and you know my body so you are the best coach I could possibly have. Body I ask for your forgiveness for any way in which I have mistreated you in the past. Jesus bring to mind any specific times where I have not treated my body with honour and respect ,so that I can release forgiveness over myself and others where necessary.

As each memory comes to mind, repent. Say sorry to God for treating His temple (you) without honour. Forgive yourself and forgive anyone that lead you to this lack of respect for your body, His temple.

Use the following prompt questions to find more freedom in these areas. Be aware of the first thing that comes to mind after you have spoken these questions to the Lord, it may be a memory, a phrase, or a picture in your mind's eye. Use the information revealed to you to commune with God. Extend forgiveness where needed and do business with God.

Jesus show me what you think of me.
Jesus am I loveable?
Jesus do I have a door open to self hatred?
Jesus when was this door first opened?
Is there anyone I need to forgive to close the door?
Is there anyone else?
What lie did I pick up from this door being ajar?
Did I learn anything else?
Do I need to do anything else in order to shut this door?

....
....
....
....
....
....

Give God any lies that you are believing and ask Him what His truth about you is, in exchange for the lies that you give him. How do you feel now?

....
....
....
....
....
....
....
....
....
....
....
....
....
....
....
....

Prayer: I accept your truth. Show me the fullness of your love for me. Jesus I choose to live in this truth and leave all lies behind me. And I break any family line that has taught me not to honour my body. I extend forgiveness to my mother and her mother and for all the generations that have not lived as princesses in your Kingdom. Today I draw a line of your blood in the sand and say it is a new day. I break away from past patterns, and start a new family value of self respect. Body I honour you. Be at peace. Jesus what is your judgement of me?

Picture again that door in your mind. Is it open or closed? (If it is still open you can spend some more time asking God to show you what else needs to be done in order for the door to close, or you can find Christian leaders you trust to help you through this process.)

> **Growth**: Baby is now 4.57 inches (11.6cm) and approximately 3.53 ounces (100gm). Fat begins to form underneath the skin. The heart is pumping as much as six gallons of blood a day and beats at a rate of about double your heart rate. Sucking, swallowing, hiccupping and blinking are now evident. Your baby has learned to breathe underwater! These actions help the lungs to develop and grow. Your baby can now co-ordinate movement.

Note: I have really struggled with morning sickness in my pregnancies but I was shown some research and watched several documentaries[4] on whole food based eating and we as a family decided to radically change our diet. Shortly after we did my morning sickness went away. The main research relating to morning sickness suggested that eating more Legumes (beans, lentils and certain peas) will help remove bile that causes the morning sickness in the first place. We made a fundamental lifestyle change that lasted longer than being pregnant and we have seen great benefits in our health and general feeling of well being. When I was pregnant, if we went back to eating a less healthy diet I would wake up the next morning with sickness. (To find the article I read on morning sickness go to karenhurd.com[5]).

 *Week 17* - **Joy**

Meditate on the following verses, mulling over their meanings:

> *Psalm 16:11 You will show me the path of life; In Your presence is fullness of joy; At Your right hand are pleasures forevermore.*

> *Proverbs 17.22 A cheerful heart is good medicine, but a crushed spirit dries up the bones.*

> *Nehemiah 8:10 ...for the joy of the LORD is your strength.*

> *Hebrews 1.9 ...therefore God, your God, has set you above your companions by anointing you with the oil of joy.*

> *Proverbs 27:19 As water reflects the face, so one's life reflects the heart.*

If you are not a naturally happy person choose to throw off the spirit of despair. Joy isn't a bouncy frolic, but an inner strength and assurance. However, happiness is a symptom of joy! A joyful heart shows a happy face. If you know you are sad or don't often show a happy face, spend time with God using the following prompt prayers. Being in His presence is where we find joy. If you ever feel yourself getting sad do a quick check on how much time you have been spending with Him.

These are the things I do where sadness can often overshadow me:

Close your eyes and wait for His presence, then ask each member of the Godhead to show you their faces: (Are they happy or sad?) Write down what you see in your mind's eye:

....
....
....

God why do I sometimes feel sad? (He may show you a specific memory of when you first started feeling this way. There may be someone you need to forgive. Forgiveness is not saying it was okay but it is releasing someone from your judgements. Unforgiveness is like drinking poison and waiting for the other person to die! It just makes you more sad!)

Jesus please come and take away my sadness: (Visualise your sadness in your hands in front of you and wait for Him to take it). God what will you give me in return for my sadness? (Wait for God to give you something. You may feel, see, sense or hear something). Write down below what He exchanged your sadness for:

....
....
....
....
....

Jesus in what ways can my home become a place of joy?

On a scale of 1-5, how joyful do you think you are?

Explain why you gave yourself this score:

Now ask a few friends "on a scale of 1-5, how joyful do you think I am?" Fill out the form with their answers:

Friend's name	Rating	Explanation

Does the contents of this table surprise you?

Knocking yourself out of a melancholic mood can be managed naturally too. What makes you happy?

This week I plan on doing this fun activity:

This week I plan on watching the following comedy movie:

Make a playlist below of 'happy' songs and have it on repeat all week:

1:

2:

3:

4:

5:

Every day this week set a timer for three minutes and just laugh out loud until it buzzes. You will feel ridiculous! But as you forget your inhibitions, take note of how laughing has made you feel:

Each day this week search for a joke on the internet that makes you chuckle. Post each one on any social networking site you are subscribed to. Write the one that made you laugh the most here:

....
....
....
....

Note below what has made you happy each day this week:

Monday

Tuesday

Wednesday

Thursday

Friday

Saturday

Sunday

Note what has happened this week after you have been in a happier environment:

....

....

Prayer: God may my life be marked by joy. May I be set apart from those around me because I am unnaturally happy and full of joy, no matter my circumstances just as you were. Jesus even though my circumstance, are sometimes poor, I know that by living in joy you will give me strength. I know that a happy heart has direct affect on my body. I choose to throw off despair and ask that you anoint me with the oil of joy. Depression I speak to you and tell you to leave, I will not experience the baby blues in Jesus name. You are my joy and you have crowned me with yours.

Growth: Baby is now 4.97 ounces (140gm) and is 5.12 inches (13cm) long. Their eyes are looking forward now, but they are still firmly closed. Meconium (made up of products of cell loss, digestive secretion and swallowed amniotic fluid) is accumulating in the bowel. This black gooey substance will become your baby's first poop! The umbilical cord is growing thicker and stronger. Baby's skeleton is changing from cartilage to bone. The bones remain flexible to make the journey through the birth canal easier.

Extra Reading: Read, (or listen to the free online audio of), 'Pollyanna' by Eleanor H Porter. It's an inspirational fictional story of a little girl who will not let any circumstance take away her joy.

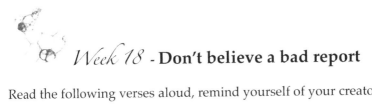 *Week 18* - **Don't believe a bad report**

Read the following verses aloud, remind yourself of your creator God.

> *Psalm 139:13 For you created my inmost being; you knit me together in my mother's womb.*

> *Genesis 1:27 So God created mankind in his own image, in the image of God He created them; male and female He created them.*

Think for a moment on what being made in the image of God would mean and note your musings below:

....

....

....

....

....

Often times we lose sight of the glory of God. People around us can be very quick to lower the standard. It may be doctors, family or friends. It could be a snide comment, expectation or medical condition. These are called bad reports that people speak over you. Our words have the power of life and death; to create and destroy. God is our creator and His standard is to bring life and perfection, to whatever He speaks.

List some 'bad reports' that have been said over you and your baby:

1:

2:

3:

4:

When people say these things I feel:

....
....

When people say the above, I do/or will do, the following:

....
....
....

Prayer: God I give you these bad reports. I choose to push out from under these negative weights and hand them to you. I forgive the people who have spoken out against me reaching your standard, I bless them, and ask you to extend grace to them. I break every negative attitude, word, and condition spoken out over me and my baby. I plead your blood to cover me, and protect me from all harm. I speak life where they have spoken negatively, forgive them for not partnering with your creative power. God set a guard on my mind to know how to filter, and process when people bring negative words. I will set my mind on things above.

Take each bad report and ask God for the truth. He may bring a scripture or testimony to mind, or tell you something directly. Write below the truth to the corresponding bad report. For example if people have told you, '*you will miscarry*' the truth could be revealed to you as, '*God promises in Malachi I will not drop my fruit before its time*'

1:

2:

3:

On a scale of 1-10, how true does each statement feel? Write your score next to each statement. These truths make me feel:

....
....
....
....
....

Jesus how can these truths become more real to me?

Are there any areas in my thinking, where I have a lower standard than what is available?

Jesus, where did I learn to have this lower standard?

Prayer: I hand you these areas of thinking. I forgive the people who taught me to think in this way and I bless them. Jesus come and renew my mind in these areas and align my thoughts with your higher ones. Holy Spirit remind me continually of my position in Heaven, and make me aware of what is available to me.

> Ephesians 6: 10-17 Finally, be strong in the Lord and in his mighty power. Put on the full armour of God, so that you can take your stand against the devil's schemes. For our struggle is not against flesh and blood, but against the rulers, against the authorities, against the powers of this dark world and against the spiritual forces of evil in the heavenly realms. Therefore put on the full armour of God, so that when the day of evil comes, you may be able to stand your ground, and after you have done everything, to stand. Stand firm then, with the belt of truth buckled around your waist, with the breastplate of righteousness in place, and with your feet fitted with the readiness that comes from the gospel of peace. In addition to all this, take up the shield of faith, with which you can extinguish all the flaming arrows of the evil one. Take the helmet of salvation and the sword of the Spirit, which is the word of God.

What things can you do to have your shield of faith active, at all times, when talking to people?
....
....

When people say these things to me I am now going to react in the following way:
....
....

When I feel rocked by what people say I will do the following to get myself back into a place of peace:

....

....

> *Proverbs 26:18-25 Like a maniac shooting flaming arrows of death is one who deceives their neighbour and says, "I was only joking!" Without wood a fire goes out; without a gossip a quarrel dies down. As charcoal to embers and as wood to fire, so is a quarrelsome person for kindling strife. The words of a gossip are like choice morsels; they go down to the inmost parts. Like a coating of silver dross on earthenware are fervent lips with an evil heart. Enemies disguise themselves with their lips, but in their hearts they harbour deceit. Though their speech is charming, do not believe them, for seven abominations fill their hearts*

When people try and lower the standard of what you are believing you need to have an inner strength that reacts. It's called faith. When people throw flames at you it can only ignite if there is wood to burn.

As we draw near to God He draws near to us. Read *Psalm 23: "He sets a table for us in the midst of our enemies."* The people who have said negative things over us are not our enemy, but the words they spoke are aligning with the enemy's plans to destroy. In Bible times, when a king was at war, he would invite neighbouring kings to come and sit at his table overlooking the battle field, before the battle commenced. The attacking army would then see the power of the force that they would be fighting, and they would see who was aligned with the king they wanted to fight. Psalm 23 is all about rest even in war. God prepares a table for us, for the principalities to see that we have a powerful King on our side, and that fighting against us would cause them much grief. At the beginning of the battle we are triumphant and can eat and rest, knowing that if God is for us then who can be against us? (Romans 8:31).

Find some bread or a cracker, some wine or juice and take communion. You have repented for not having the mind of Christ and you are reminding yourself of what He has done and the position you now have in Him. As you eat with your King you make the declaration that you have aligned with Christ and you will win the war. It's a victory meal.

Prayer: God I know that you are knitting and making my baby within me. I am confident that you do all things well. My body and my baby are created in your image, you are perfect and therefore my baby and I are perfectly made. You have no intention of harming me or my baby. I stand assured that you have plans only to prosper us. I actively put up my shield of faith, and put on your full armour. I will stand in a place of intercession for my baby and declare a positive outcome to any negativity that I face. I draw my strength from you, and will stand strong when people say negative things, I will believe you, and your word above anything else I am told.

Growth: Prenatal vitamins are important to help your placenta feed the baby. Baby's vocal chords are formed and they go through the motions of crying but without air no sound is made. The external ear can be clearly seen on an ultrasound. Your baby measures about 5.59 inches (14.2cm) this week and weighs about 6.7 ounces (190gm).

Extra reading: Judges 5:3, 2 Samuel 22:50, 1 Chronicles 16:9, 2 Chronicles 5:13, Psalm 30:12, Psalm 33:3, Psalm 59:16, Psalm 68:4. Pray a worshipper's heart over your baby. Read the life of David, a man after God's own heart. Pray for your child's voice, the tone, the strength, and the range.

# Week 19 - Butterflies

I first felt you move when:

When you moved I felt:

....
....

I do/don't want to find out if you are a boy or a girl because:

I think you are a: ...
Because:

> *Deuteronomy 26:9-11 He brought us to this place and gave us this land, a land flowing with milk and honey; and now I bring the firstfruits of the soil that you, LORD, have given me. Place the basket before the LORD your God and bow down before him. Then you and the Levites and the foreigners residing among you shall rejoice in all the good things the LORD your God has given to you and your household.*

You now have confirmation, of the promise of a child God has given you, as you feel the baby move. These movements are the first fruits of the promise. Come before Him with your first fruits. Bow before Him, worship and release what is in your heart to pray.

Prayer: God I thank you for bringing me to this land of pregnancy and thank you for the fruit of this baby. I praise you that I am well and that you continually provide for me. I offer you what you have accomplished in me, this new life. I present this baby to you, safely tucked in the basket of my womb. Let the midwives, doctors, my friends and relatives marvel at the good things you have done.

Write a list of promises that God gave you about your life that you have now seen fulfilled

1:

2:

3:

> Zechariah 4:10 "Who dares despise the day of small things, since the seven eyes of the LORD that range throughout the earth will rejoice when they see..."

Write below some promises that you have been given, but have not yet been fulfilled:

Write a list of promises for this pregnancy, labour and the life of your baby:

....

....

....

....

....

Don't despise the day of small beginnings but be thankful. Thankfulness, even in small things, brings a kingdom increase. We can be thankful because we are in faith. Thankfulness is the evidence that a person has received what they are believing for. And thankfulness is the attitude in which it is possible to stay in faith as you align your reality with that of heaven. Thankfulness shows faith, because you can only be thankful when you believe the promises you have been given will definitely happen. 'Your kingdom come your will be done.' If we want more of Him in our life, thankfulness is a key. Your disposition changes and you position yourself to receive.

What things can you be thankful for this week, even if they seem tiny?

> *Colossians 2:6-7 So then, just as you received Christ Jesus as Lord, continue to live your lives in Him, rooted and built up in Him, strengthened in the faith as you were taught, and overflowing with thankfulness.*

From your lists, take time to thank God for His promises; ones that you have seen and ones that you are yet to see the fulfilment of. Note how you feel once you have pondered and spoken aloud His goodness:

....

....

....

If you are experiencing negative symptoms like morning sickness, look for the things each day that you can be glad about. If you are less sick today than yesterday, change your speech into thankfulness, *"thank you that I am less sick today."* Be thankful that you see improvement or if you are about the same as yesterday, be thankful that you are no worse. Focus on the good rather than on the circumstances. Then declare over tomorrow. As you are thankful today your outlook for tomorrow changes, your faith increases and so does the outcome of your circumstances; *"Tomorrow I speak out even less sickness than today, increase your standard in my body. From glory to glory."*

Prayer: God help me to be thankful in all things. God I thank you so much that this baby has begun to move and I take hold of that as a first fruit of the promise of this baby coming. I will not despise the day of small beginnings. I stand on your promises and thank you for them because I know that you are not a man that you can lie. I thank you for the remainder of this pregnancy, I thank you for health, I thank you that I will see your goodness and faithfulness to me. Thank you for giving me a support system. Thank you for good resources to help me keep in your presence. Thank you for the correct staff at my birth. Thank you for your presence. Thank you for your unfailing love. Thank you for renewing my mind. Thank you for giving me faith. Thank you that you take me from glory to glory. Thank you for all the miracles I have heard about and witnessed. Thank you for journeying with me, thank you that you have promised that you will never leave me. Thank you for making my path straight. Thank you for giving me hope.

Continue to thank the Lord for anything that springs up inside you. Notice how you feel after being thankful for just a few minutes.

....
....
....
....
....
....
....
....
....
....
....
....
....
....
....
....
....

Growth: Your baby has the same waking and sleeping patterns of a new born, and has a favourite position for sleep and recognisable active and rest periods. Throughout your baby's body, nerves are being coated with a fatty substance called myelin, which insulates the nerves so that impulses can flow smoothly. If your baby is female her uterus starts to develop. Her vagina, uterus, and fallopian tubes are all in place. She has approximately six million eggs in her ovaries. About one million will remain at birth. If it's a boy, the genitals are distinct and recognisable. Your baby is swallowing amniotic fluid and the kidneys are making urine. Your little one's size is around 6.02 inches (15.3cm) and 8.47 ounces (240gm).

 *Week 20* - **Preparing**

There are many ways in which we need to prepare for a baby. We need to prepare financially. We need to prepare the nursery room, clothes and baby food. We also need to prepare ourselves for parenthood, emotionally and spiritually, as well as practically.

> *Matthew 6:31-33 So do not worry, saying, "What shall we eat?" or "What shall we drink?" or "What shall we wear?" For the pagans run after all these things, and your heavenly Father knows that you need them. But seek first his kingdom and his righteousness, and all these things will be given to you as well.*

It is by seeking His kingdom and righteousness that all the issues of our life are sorted out, without us getting stressed over them. To seek means to *'be in quest for,'* or to go after and search out His kingdom and righteousness. It is our responsibility to actively seek out God and His Kingdom. When we seek this, our lives go well for us.

I am seeking His kingdom by:

What is righteousness? To seek righteousness we need to know what we are looking for! Do a word study of *'righteous'*, look up its meaning in a Dictionary and Thesaurus. Write its definition in the space below and highlight the words that stick out to you:

....

....

....

....

....

....

In what ways do I live righteously?

In what ways do I not live righteously?

> John 14:2-4 "My Father's house has many rooms; if that were not so, would I have told you that I am going there to prepare a place for you? And if I go and prepare a place for you, I will come back and take you to be with me that you also may be where I am. You know the way to the place where I am going."

We know the way to the place that Jesus has prepared for us. That means we can go there! In Him we find rest. Jesus died to make a way for us to go to Heaven where He has prepared a place for us (Ephesians 2:6). I don't believe that this is only talking about death. God has raised us up with Christ, and we are already seated in heavenly places, in the place that He has prepared. Jesus has come back for us, from death when He rose again, and we now have access to the place He has prepared through that act. As we prepare for our baby, we need to know that rest should mark us, not a continual striving to get things done. Rest comes from our perspective. As we are seated in heavenly places it is easier to understand His rest, and the reality of Heaven. Peace should be all about our person, because peace is all about Heaven. Our focus is not on where the money is coming from to pay for all the new equipment we need but our focus is on Him. All the money we need is in His kingdom. If we seek and strive for money we won't find it, but if we seek Him, He gives us what we need. We seek Him from our heavenly perspective of Him and in so doing He adds to us all that we need.

I feel that my awareness of my heavenly position affects my preparation by:

On a scale of one to ten, how assured are you that God is working all things together for your good? (One = striving on my own to get things done. Ten = fully understanding that all the best things come from His kingdom.) ...

Using the same scale how prepared do you feel to be a parent? ...

For the baby's room I have bought:

I have been given:

I need:

This is the way I feel about how much I have got done so far:

I have prepared myself for motherhood by:

On a scale of 1-10 I feel prepared;

Spiritually:

Physically:

Emotionally:

I need to do the following to improve these scores:

Prayer: Holy Spirit teach me your ways, show me Jesus. Prepare my heart, mind, soul and body for the journey ahead. Make me more aware of my heavenly position. Pull me out of my circumstances and show me what you see. Let me rest in the finished work of your cross. And help me grasp that you have prepared everything for me. I rest knowing you work all things together for me because of this love relationship we have together. You are a good Father and you will give me more than what I need, you will give me the desires of my heart. So I give to you all worry I have about paying for all the new things I will need for my new arrival. I trust you. Prepare the best bargains for me, let me be in the right place at the right time to see the best items. Let me be wise in my choices but not succumb to a poverty mindset. Holy Spirit guide me into all truth, even knowing what I will need.

Growth: The rapid growth stage is about over. The baby's heart grows stronger. The legs are reaching their relative size. Immunities you have built up are being transferred from you to your baby. These immune cells will protect your baby from viruses you've already had for up to six months after birth! The nerve cells in the brain for taste, smell, hearing, seeing, and touch are now developing. Baby is about 6.46 inches (16.4cm) and weighs around 10.58 ounces (300g).

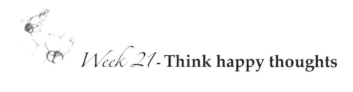

Week 21- Think happy thoughts

> *Philippians 4:8 Finally, brethren, whatever things are true, whatever things are noble, whatever things are just, whatever things are pure, whatever things are lovely, whatever things are of good report, if there is any virtue and if there is anything praiseworthy—meditate on these things.*

Write out below things that are going well with you:
(If at any stage you find yourself starting to head into negativity, you can choose to think about these things, exchanging negative thoughts with happy ones! Keep a list of things like this handy so you can pull it out on the bus or at work when you need to, it will remind you of how bad it isn't!)

....
....
....
....

Generally how positive do you think you are on a scale of 1-10?

> *Proverbs 17:22 A cheerful heart is good medicine, but a crushed spirit dries up the bones.*

How cheerful is your heart? (*Circle as appropriate*).

Not at all   Some   Very   Bursting

Proverbs is clear that when we are happy it makes us healthy. It's also medical opinion that happy people are more healthy. If you're thinking and dwelling on negative things then negativity will cloud your mind. We need to create new thought patterns in our minds that in turn make our hearts cheerful, so that we can have life in abundance. It's out of the overflow of our hearts that we speak. Listen to yourself talk to people this week and discover what you are really in faith for.

Proverbs 23:7 For as he thinks in his heart, so is he. (NKJ)

Spend a few minutes in His presence then evaluate what is in your heart. Proverbs tells us that it is what is in our minds and our hearts, that shows us who we really are. Be honest with yourself. Are you happy? Do you rejoice always? Are you peaceful? Are you playful? Are you positive? Are you loving? Write below a brief evaluation about yourself and note what, if anything, you intend to do about what you have discovered:

....
....
....
....
....
....
....
....
....
....
....
....
....
....
....

Luke 6:45 A good man brings good things out of the good stored up in his heart, and an evil man brings evil things out of the evil stored up in his heart. For the mouth speaks what the heart is full of.

In Greek, the word *heart*[7] includes your mind, or your thinking. So then our mouths say what we are thinking about. What percentage of the day do you have on your mind the items on the list below, tick as appropriate.

In a day I think about...	0%	10%	25%	50%	75%	100%
The chores you need to do:						
The future:						
Scripture:						

In a day I think about...	0%	10%	25%	50%	75%	100%
Family:						
God:						
Past experiences:						
Worrying:						
My baby:						
Labour:						

Looking at the above table, is there anything that you think needs to be readdressed?:

....

....

....

....

....

....

....

....

....

....

....

....

....

....

....

....

....

....

....

....

Prayer: God, this week I will consciously decide to think on things above. I will throw off all negative thoughts and only think on what is good, pure, lovely, just, virtuous, praiseworthy, noble and true.   If my circumstances say otherwise I will still choose to look to you, seated in Heaven. I will look on all that is pleasant and find peace in you.   Holy Spirit, please nudge me when I start to think negatively. My Soul, I speak to you, bless the Lord this week. God, forgive me for all my negativity, make me into a positive person. I declare I will see your goodness. I will see your promises to me fulfilled. I will see your joyous expression. My soul will find rest in your presence. I will turn my thoughts and affection towards you.

Growth: White blood cells are under production, they form our body's defence system. They help fight infections and diseases. Your little one's skin has changed from translucent to more opaque. Your infant's tongue is fully formed. Wake and sleep periods become more consistent. Some research suggests, that your baby sets its internal clock to match the outside worlds even before birth; Your eating and sleeping habits as well levels of light and noise serve as signals for this developing routine. Length is now measured crown to heel. Baby measures about 10.51 inches (26.7cm) and weighs nearly 12.7 ounces (360g).

Extra thoughts: Take some time to pray over your baby, that as they begin to set their clock to the outside world they will never loose sight of heavenly habits, times, and seasons. That they will never struggle with the concept of dual citizenship with earth and Heaven.

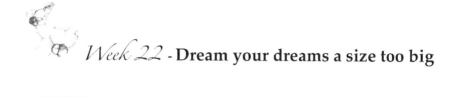

Week 22 - **Dream your dreams a size too big**

> *Ephesians 3:20 Now to him who is able to do immeasurably more than all we ask or imagine, according to his power that is at work within us.*

Internally read over Ephesians 3:20 three times, then another three times speak it aloud to yourself. Sit quietly for a while and ponder what you have asked God to do in this pregnancy, during your labour and for the life of your child.

Write below a list of what you have asked of Him:

....
....
....
....
....

Set an alarm to ring in five minutes' time. Now let yourself imagine; imagine what the rest of your pregnancy could look like. Imagine what your labour could be like. Imagine the kind of mother you would like to be, and what your child will be like and grow to become. You may like to put on some music while you do this.

Write below what you imagined:

....
....
....
....
....

What did you imagine your child to be and look like?:

....
....

What did you imagine a good birth to be like for you?:

....
....
....
....
....

Write what you imagine a good mother looks like and how you want to parent:

....
....
....
....
....
....

Psalm 37:4 Delight yourself also in the LORD, and He shall give you the desires of your heart.

As we allow ourselves time to dream and imagine, in the presence of God our dreams turn into reality. God wants you to reach for and obtain all that is in your heart. He is interested in your success. He didn't create you to fail but to flourish spectacularly! So if God is for us who can be against us? (Romans 8:31.) Our own fears and mind-sets hold us back. We need to renew our minds into a new way of thinking where all our dreams are not only do-able, but are likely to happen. So write below what you want to ask the Lord concerning pregnancy, birth and motherhood:

....
....
....
....
....
....
....
....
....
....

....
....
....
....

Note: Be aware of what is bubbling in your heart when you ask. Are you in anguish for something? Are you at peace or in fear? Really examine where your expectations are. How much do your expectations match up with what you have imagined in the questions above? Find His peace and ask Him to take your fear. You need to deal with these fears, don't ignore them. For your dreams to be reached, obstacles of fear need to be cleared away.

Close your eyes and spend some time with God pondering the following prompt questions. (Process the answers in your mind or on a separate piece of paper as you don't need to keep a record of negative things).

Jesus, do I have a door to fear open in my life?

Jesus, when did this door to fear first get opened?

Jesus, who do I need to forgive in order for this access point to shut? (Forgive who comes to mind. It doesn't excuse the wrong done to you, but forgiveness sets you free).

Speak this out loud: Jesus, as I hand to you fear, I speak over myself freedom from fear and I break all agreements I have made with the spirit of fear. Jesus I give you control of my life. Father I thank you that you are big enough to protect me.

Jesus, what lie did I learn from letting fear in?

Jesus, I give you that lie and ask you to forgive me for believing it. I forgive those who taught me the lie. Jesus, will you now show me the truth in exchange? Write down the truth God gave you:

If there are more areas of fear that you are aware of, take each one to Him, name it out loud, "Jesus I am fearful, anxious or worried about..." "I give it to you and forgive those who taught me to fear these things. What is your truth for me?" List out the truths below:

1.

2.

3.

4.

5.

Read these truths out loud to yourself, "I now believe that..." each day this week.

Prayer: God help me to be a big dreamer. Holy Spirit draw me away to be with you so that I can get a new perspective on my life, one from a heavenly viewpoint. I choose to delight myself in you, whatever my current walk, I know that you are good and I will be glad because I know you. God I want to be close to you, so that my desires come in line with your good and pleasing will for me. Holy Spirit come with your power and be at work within me. Make me aware of my great destiny in you. Father come and help me realise that you are for me, show me if there is anything in my own mind working against me. Jesus help me to renew my mind, I want to think the way you do, even about myself.

Growth: Your baby can now hear your conversations more clearly than before. When you talk, read, or sing, expect your baby to hear you. Studies have found that newborns will suck more vigorously when read to from a book they heard frequently in utero. Eyelids and eyebrows are fully formed. Fingernails have grown to the end of the fingers. If your baby is male his testes begin their descent to the scrotum. Primitive sperm have formed and he is producing testosterone. Length is 10.94 inches (27.8cm); weight is nearly 1 pound (430gm).

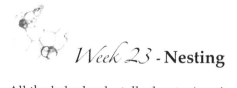 *Week 23* - **Nesting**

All the baby books talk about a 'nesting' time. Your hormones are reacting in preparation for your baby and suddenly you may feel an urge to paint or spring clean.

I personally never had a reaction like this. I am a fairly practical and organised person. I cleaned and stacked all the cloths well before time, I think once my body did kick into any nesting period everything was already done! Having said that, looking back particularly on my first pregnancy, I realise there was a certain amount of clinical process, rather than emotional mothering, involved in my journey. I was ecstatic when I found I was pregnant in a lunch break at work, a warm fuzzy feeling welled up and I immediately put my hands to my stomach and prayed over my new child. I was not completely devoid of emotion, and if asked I wouldn't have realised how emotionless I felt, but looking back now I can see how rigid I was. I have never been a very open person; for me not showing too many emotions was normal. After the birth of my second child I realised that first time round something had been lacking.

I want to talk about bonding: it's something that most people think is automatic. It probably should be, but for me it wasn't. When my daughter was born the midwives placed her onto my chest, I briefly looked down at her happily, but I was exhausted from the lengthy pushing stage. All I wanted to do was rest. I encouraged my husband, Luke, to take her as soon as I was recovered enough to go and take a shower. The midwives clearly wanted me to hold her as much as possible, I needed stitches so they lay her in my arm to distract me. Again I wanted Luke to hold her so I could focus. Don't get me wrong, I loved her immediately, "I can't believe she's mine," is what I said, but it was not an overwhelming emotional charge.

The next day my parents came for dinner and we decided to get a takeaway. I wanted to stretch my legs, so slowly my husband, dad and I walked to the local Chinese. It was only when my Mom mentioned it as we got back, that I realised I had left my Mom in charge without even thinking that this was the first time we'd left our daughter! A few days later my Mom quietly said to me, "Don't forget to just hold her." It irritated me at the time! I was following my routine. I thought I was doing everything just fine, thank you very much! But what she said eventually sunk in and I realised that I never sat and just watched my baby sleep, or let her fall asleep in my arms for long periods of time.

This information all pulled together for me shortly after our son's birth, our second child. As I picked him out of the water and held him in my arms, a deep burst of emotion exploded within me. He was mine and I gushed about how gorgeous he was. It was an immediate bond. Something had welled up inside of me from my core. It was like I had been missing him my whole life! The emotion I felt was an unstoppable force. It was an entirely different experience the second time around. Now, I love to cuddle up to both my kids and I get a mushy feeling when they snuggle up, I could watch them both sleep all night.

I'm still pragmatic with an introverted personality, not showing everyone my gooey side. But for me something had obviously changed between pregnancies. I can only put that down to a stronger relationship with God. I have dealt with personal paradigms and certain mindsets that disallowed my emotions to function properly. I did this through God exposing to me what He was really like through His Word, through personal ministry and self assessment. Through knowing God and knowing myself. You may not have the same protectors in place as I did in front of my emotions, but you will have other areas in your life that do not look like Jesus. Salvation is a process that we are all on. We must deal with the parts of us that are not yet living in the fullness of our redeemed nature as we spend time in His presence seeking His face. When we see Him we are transformed into His image.

Use the following questions as a springboard. Answer the question and then take the answer to the Lord and process it with Him. Ask God if anything needs to be worked through. To mother well we need to experience personal freedom first. To be a place of safety and rest for our child, we need to take care of our rough edges, and process out the things that don't belong, the bits of us that are not like Jesus. Go through each question and see what the Lord reveals. Use the questions as a starting point, ask more of your own and really engage with Him. Start by closing your eyes and wait until you attune yourself to His surrounding presence. How do you feel in this moment?:

....
....
....

What has made you feel this way?:

....
....
....

If I were to ask you to picture each of the Godhead in turn, where would they be in the room?
Father God:
Jesus:
Holy Spirit:
Note how where you are seeing the Godhead in your picture makes you feel:

What emotion rose up when you found out you were pregnant?:

When I think about mothering in the same way as I was mothered, these emotions bubble up:

My relationship with my own mother is:

If I was braver, this is what I would say to my mother:

Jesus, do I need to forgive my mum for anything?

Jesus, is there a lie I believe about Holy Spirit through the way I've been mothered?

Jesus, I hand to you the lie that...

What truth do you have for me in exchange?

Picture Holy Spirt again, *now* what is your picture of Him?

In an emotional situation how do I usually respond?

Jesus, do I let myself feel emotion freely?

If I find myself needing to cry I:

I do/don't feel comfortable laughing out loud because:

Do I let people help me?

Do I show people if I am vulnerable?

Jesus, do I have a wall up to protect me from getting hurt in my emotions?

Is there anyone I need to forgive in order for this wall to be brought down?

Jesus, is it safe for me to take this wall down?

What will protect me if I do?

Jesus, will you come and take the wall down now, or can I do it myself?: (Wait until you feel/sense/see the wall is gone).

What other barriers do I have in place? (If any more pictures of walls or barriers come to mind, or you think of a word such as fear or isolation, ask Jesus if it is safe to take the wall of fear or isolation down).

When I think about looking after a baby, this is how I feel?

I feel prepared for this baby in the following ways:

I feel unprepared in these ways:

How have I already bonded with my baby?

On a scale of 1-10 how bonded do I feel with my baby: (1= not at all, 10=totally enraptured) ...

Imagining a score of ten out of ten for the last question describe what that would look like in practice:

....
....

....

....

....

....

....

Write one thing you can do in the next twenty four hours to take a step towards this outcome:

Jesus is there anything I need to deal with so that I can bond with my baby better?:

Pregnancy is all about preparation. We prepare our houses for a new arrival. We may change our lifestyle and our mind-sets. But we must remember, that in the midst of all our preparing, that Jesus has prepared a place for us. (As we touched on in "Week 20 Preparing".) It's a place where we can be with Him and not have to strive. As you begin this week, schedule in times of rest for you to be with Jesus.

Write out the following verse and put it where you can see it. Meditate on it this week until you know that He is your refuge. Speak it out repeatedly until you know that you trust Him:

> *Psalm 91:1-2 Whoever dwells in the shelter of the Most High will rest in the shadow of the Almighty. I will say of the LORD, "He is my refuge and my fortress, my God, in whom I trust."*

'Nesting' is not only an instinct for us towards our baby but we must also find our place in Him; rested and nestled under His wing. It's in His shelter that we become a safe place for our families. We don't have to have it all together if we position ourselves in Him. We often protect ourselves with various coping mechanisms but the most healthy way to self-protect is to let Him protect us, as we rest in His mighty strength.

On a scale of 1-10, how much do I trust God for the birth I am expecting to experience?

When you read the statement from *Psalm 91:1-2*, *"He is my refuge and my fortress, my God, in whom I trust."* How true does it feel to you personally?

The more that we get to know someone, the more we can trust them to protect us. You cannot trust who you do not know. It's from a place of intimacy that He becomes our safe place.

I intend to meet with God in the following ways this week:

I intend to do this at the following times this week:

These are the ways I '*dwell with God*':

These are the ways I need to *dwell with God'*:

While you're making time with God this week put on some worship, or soaking style music and ask God to encounter you like never before. What aspect of God do you want to know more of?

....
....
....
....

Ask Him to reveal Himself to you in a new way. Write what He has revealed to you:

....
....
....
....
....
....
....
....
....
....
....
....
....
....
....
....
....
....
....
....
....
....
....
....
....
....

Prayer: Jesus help me make time for you this week. Draw me away. Let me rest under the shelter of your wing. Help me to prepare for the arrival of this baby, but also help me to prepare myself more fully in you. I know that all things come from you, so I place myself in you. I trust you. I will dwell with you. God I want to end this journey of pregnancy knowing you like never before. Expose in me areas that do not reflect you. I draw aside to know you better. I will delight myself in you, and throw off the former things. I will throw off all that tries to entangle me and run this race into mothering. God I offer you all my earthly ability to mother well, I lay my efforts on your altar and ask for you to supernaturally empower me to be the best mother I can be. Holy Spirit teach me to mother from your perspective. I choose to bless my own mother and grandmother, I ask you God to open my eyes to any incorrect methods, to draw from the good and ignore the obscure.

Write down five attributes, or characteristics, that you feel you know of God, and note how you learnt them.

1:

2:

3:

4:

5:

Now list three things of God that you feel you know or experience personally the least or that you would like to understand more fully.

1:

2:

3:

Growth: Proportions of the body are now quite similar to a newborn, although thinner, since baby hasn't begun to form body fat. Bones located in the middle ear harden. Your baby is able to hear. (Dads, did you know: low-frequency sounds mimicking a male voice penetrate the abdomen and uterine wall better than the higher frequencies of the female voice?) The eyes are formed, though the iris still lacks pigmentation. The average baby at this stage weighs 1.1 pound (501gm) and is 11.38 inches (28.9cm) long.

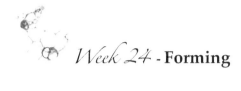 *Week 24* - **Forming**

Being pregnant I have noticed people treat me:

We had the second scan on:

Now I know you are a boy / girl I feel:

When daddy found out he:

We still haven't found out if you're a boy or girl because:

When we saw you in the scan we felt:

When we saw you, you were:

> Psalm 139:14-16 *I praise you because I am fearfully and wonderfully made; your works are wonderful, I know that full well. My frame was not hidden from you when I was made in the secret place, when I was woven together in the depths of the earth. Your eyes saw my unformed body; all the days ordained for me were written in your book before one of them came to be.*

How does knowing God is watching your baby make you feel?

....
....
....
....
....

Ask God what He sees when He's looking at your baby:

....
....
....
....
....
....
....
....
....
....
....
....
....
....
....
....
....
....
....
....
....
....
....
....

> *Jeremiah 1:12 The LORD said to me, "You have seen correctly, for I am watching to see that my word is fulfilled."*

Conception is a promise. It's a promise of a baby; it's the beginning of life. God is watching over each seed of promise to see it grow.

Write a list below, of all the parts of your baby that are still to form over the next seventeen weeks, and speak life over each area. Speaking life is more than positive thought or speech, our words carry the power to create. For example speak out over your baby, declaring it into being. "Lungs. I speak to you lungs and tell you to grow well. Be formed correctly and in proper time. Baby I speak over you, that you will have a good set of lungs. Lungs I bless you and say that you will never be compromised by asthma, hay fever, allergy or accident. Baby you will speak well from an early age and sing beautifully, people will sit up and listen to what you have to say, the very breath of God will be upon the words you speak and sing."

1:

2:

3:

4:

5:

At the scan the doctors told us:

This has made me:

If the doctors have told you that not everything is well, write below what you are now going to do:

> *Galatians 3:13 Christ redeemed us from the curse of the law by becoming a curse for us, for it is written: "Cursed is everyone who is hung on a pole."*

Jesus became a curse for us so that we do not need to live under it. The curse brought suffering and ill health. It lowered the perfect standard. But we are now redeemed. You and your baby can live free from sickness and disease. The standard has been reinstated. We can now see His face in heavenly places. His name, one that carries healing, is written on our foreheads. He has marked us with His good name. His name carries authority and we are marked with it.

> *Revelation 22:3-4 No longer will there be any curse. The throne of God and of the Lamb will be in the city, and his servants will serve him. They will see his face, and his name will be on their foreheads.*

Prayer: God I know that you see my baby. I know that you show yourself strong on their behalf. My baby is free from the curse, because I am free from the curse, because I accept Jesus. My baby can grow under your watchful eye. Baby you are fearfully and wonderfully made. I speak shalom (Meaning: Peace, meaning, nothing missing, nothing broken) over you baby. I speak Shalom over my body. Jesus I know that you will continue this good work you have started and form my baby into perfection.

Growth: Baby gains about 6 ounces this week, the weight is in muscle, bone mass and organs. Taste buds begin to form. This week the sweat glands will be forming in the skin. The lungs are developing. The baby's skin is pink, wrinkled and translucent. Rapid eye movements can be seen and baby may have a blink startle reaction to your sudden movements or noises. Baby weighs 1.3 pound (600gm) and is 11.8 inches (30cm) long.

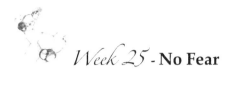

Week 25 - **No Fear**

> *Isaiah 41:10 Fear not, for I am with you; be not dismayed, for I am your God. I will strengthen you, yes, I will help you, I will uphold you with My righteous right hand.'*

Generally I would class myself as a fearful / un-fearful person because:

These are some of the areas where I feel afraid or anxious, therefore I know I do not trust God enough:

1:

2:

3:

When I think about my labour I feel worried or apprehensive in the following areas:

....
....
....
....
....
....
....

When I think about being a mother I feel nervous in the following areas:

....
....
....

....
....
....
....

If you have answered anything in the questions above, then it's likely that you have a door to fear open in your life. Let's close that access point and see what God's truth is for you in those areas.

Jesus, when did the door to fear first get opened in my life?

Is there someone I need to forgive in order to close the door?

What lies have I learnt whilst being under the influence of fear?

1:

2:

3:

Spend time with God and process the above questions. Be honest with God and ask more direct questions as needed. Once you have done so, place your hands in front of you and visualise all the fear you have, in all its various forms such as nerves, anxiety, worry, unease, being poured into your hands. Speak out loud and renounce the lies that you have believed. "I give you the lie that I need to be fearful in this particular area, I choose no longer to partner with it." Lift your hands up and ask out loud that Jesus will take all of the fear and all of the lies away. Wait until you feel He has done so. Take a deep breath and realise that you are now a different person, a fearless person. Trust that Jesus has done as you asked and taken all fear from you, leaving you free. Now with your hands still in front of you ask God to give you something in return for your fear. Wait and see what He gives you.

When I gave Jesus my fear He gave me this in return:

....
....
....

Now ask Jesus to replace each lie you renounced with a truth one by one. List the truths below:

1:

2:

3:

I know that God loves me because:

....
....
....
....

Jesus, is the door to fear now closed or is there any more forgiveness or lies that I need to deal with? (If anything comes to mind continue to process with God).

Write out the following verse and put it somewhere you can see it:

> *2 Timothy 1:7 For God has not given us a spirit of fear, but of power and of love and of a sound mind.*

Speak it out loud over yourself ten times, each day this week. As you speak over yourself that you have a new fearless mind, a shift takes place in your brain and you actually become less fearful. You have renewed your mind into a new thought pattern.

> 1 John 4:18 *"There is no fear in love [dread does not exist], but full-grown (complete, perfect) love turns fear out of doors and expels every trace of terror! For fear brings with it the thought of punishment, and [so] he who is afraid has not reached the full maturity of love [is not yet grown into love's complete perfection]." (AMP)*

His love is what casts out all fear. Spend at least one minute three times a day this week, closing your eyes and letting His love wash over you. Do that now, close your eyes and ask God to wash you with His presence.

What did you perceive:

....
....
....
....
....
....
....
....

Do a word study of *'love'*. Write below the verses you find about love from the Bible:

....
....
....
....

If I asked you to close your eyes and picture Father God, what is your imagined picture of Him?

Make a mental note of His expression, the distance you are to Him. Are you afraid of Him? Do you fear His punishment? Is it a natural connection, or do you feel awkward? If I asked you to skip towards Him, jump into His lap and wrap your arms around Him, how would that make you feel?

All wrath was poured out on Jesus, He was punished so that we don't have to be. His love is all encompassing of us. Regardless of the natural example of fathering displayed to us by our own fathers, Father God wants to connect with us on every level, as a child and a mature son. It is to be an easy, secure, happy and safe place for us to be. Is that how you feel before Him?

Jesus, do I fear the Father's wrath?

Why do I believe the Father has punishment for me?

Think for a moment of the relationship you have with your earthly Father. Is it possible that you are projecting parts of what you have with your Dad on to Daddy God?

Jesus, I choose to forgive my earthly Father for:

Write a mental list of all the negative attributes or ways of thinking that your earthly father portrayed to you. Forgiveness does not say that the person was right in their actions. It does not excuse them but it gets us out of the way so that justice can be served. If we harbour even the smallest amount of unforgiveness, it festers deep within us until it becomes bitterness. We lock ourselves in prison and forgiveness is the key to freedom. Forgiveness is a command. As you choose to obey, your heart will often catch up and you then begin to feel forgiveness. You may have a great relationship with your Dad, but list the areas you see in him that do not mimic that of the word of God. For example, the Bible says Father God sings and dances over us, did your dad do that? If not then choose to forgive Him for not imitating Father God in that way.

Jesus I choose to release my Father from my judgements and to bless him where he has done me wrong. I forgive him. I renounce the lie that you Father God would treat me in the same way as my earthy Father.

Now go back and have a look at your Father God picture in your imagination. Has it changed? Do you feel different?

Note here what has happened:

....
....
....
....
....
....
....
....
....
....
....
....
....

Father God, what do you think about me?

....
....
....
....
....
....
....
....
....
....
....

Psalm 103:17 "But from everlasting to everlasting the LORD's love is with those who fear Him, and His righteousness with their children's children."

There is one kind of healthy fear. The fear of God Himself. Not because you are scared that He might hurt you: that is not God. Fear of this kind means awe or reverence. So God loves those that are in awe of Him: those that honour Him, and in turn He gives righteousness to their children. When we stand before God with our fears and worries, we make them bigger than our understanding of who He is. Our mundane fear replaces our honour and awe of God. Unhealthy fear replaces our fear of God. He is big enough to give us strength. We are to bring our fears to Him - but as we see Him, our fear becomes nothing as we see how able He is.

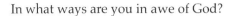

In what ways are you in awe of God?

Write specific moments where you have thought of God and been in awe of Him:

How can you honour Him more in your day to day life?

Prayer: Love reach full maturity in me so that I know no fear. God I seek you and I will find you. I draw near to you, and you draw near to me. I will seek to know you better, as I know you, I know your love for me. Father overwhelm me with your love. Release over me fresh experiences of your love. Jesus I choose to press into you. I choose to look at you and not my fear. Fear I tell you to leave in the name of Jesus. I take the authority given to me by Jesus and tell you fear, have no place in me. I clothe myself in love. God I look to you. You are awesome, and bigger than all my worry. I choose to honour you and not glorify this fear any longer. Take the true place of honour in my life.

Growth: The structures of the spine begin to form, joints, ligaments and rings; These will protect the spinal cord. Blood vessels of the lungs develop. Your baby's nostrils begin to open. The nerves around the mouth and lip area are now more sensitive. Their swallowing reflexes are developing. Your child has now obtained an approximate length of 13.6 inches (34.6cm) and weighs 1.46 pound (660gm).

Week 26 - **Staying focused**

> *Hebrews 12: 1-3 Therefore, since we are surrounded by such a great cloud of witnesses, let us throw off everything that hinders and the sin that so easily entangles. And let us run with perseverance the race marked out for us, fixing our eyes on Jesus, the pioneer and perfecter of faith. For the joy set before Him He endured the cross, scorning its shame, and sat down at the right hand of the throne of God. Consider Him who endured such opposition from sinners, so that you will not grow weary and lose heart.*

The Bible tells us that there is a great cloud of witnesses; I believe they cheer us on. How does this spur you on when you think about them looking down on your walk of faith?

When you think of Heaven looking down on you, how do you feel?

How do you view yourself journeying on a faith path through pregnancy? Do you feel you are doing well? Do you feel overwhelmed or at the top of your game?

How do you think Heaven, with it's great cloud of witnesses, is viewing your journey through pregnancy?

Jesus, how do you see me?

....
....
....
....
....
....
....

Does your opinion of yourself match with that of Heaven's of you?

If not ask Jesus why not. Jesus, why do I have a low opinion of myself?

Is there anyone you need to forgive for teaching you to have low self esteem? If so do so now. Forgive yourself also.

Jesus, forgive me that I have a depleted opinion of myself compared to your opinion of me. I forgive myself for not reaching my own high expectations and I release myself from the bar that I have created. I forgive myself for not staying focused and for beating myself up for any failure. I forgive myself for not believing in myself and Jesus I hand to you perfectionism and low self esteem.

Remind yourself by writing a short paragraph on what you're focused on: for pregnancy, birth and motherhood:

....
....
....
....
....

....
....
....
....
....

I find it easy/hard to stay focused on what I need to do because:

....
....

What distracts from staying focused on the task set before you? (i.e. things, people, or comments distract you

....
....

During the day I find myself thinking about: *(Tick as appropriate)*

	My baby	My labour	Scriptures	God	Other things
Never					
Not much (10% of the day)					
Often (30%)					
A lot (50%)					
All the time (90%)					

Fill out the next table. What do you think hinders you in your journey of faith-filled pregnancy? Take time to repent before God. Jesus has made the way clear for us; it is us who put blockers in our own way. 'Repent' just means to turn from what you have been doing and thinking, and walk the opposite way. From your list, talk with God about why you think in certain ways. Let Him renew your mind. You can hand Him each hindrance, and ask Him for a new way of thinking in that area.

Thought patterns and obstacles that hinder me	God's new way of thinking for me	My thoughts on this

It is sin that also entangles us (Hebrews 12:1-3). Sin is not only the obvious short-coming we think of, but sin is simply us walking out something that our unrenewed minds think of as normal. Sin in essence is anything that does not look like us living in the fullness of what Jesus has won for us. We do not need to get heavy about sin, we just need to become aware of our default setting that comes from unrenewed areas, acknowledge them, repent and believe His truth. Spend a minute and ask God if there are areas in your heart and mind that fall short of what He has won for you. Repent and then ask God for the truth.

How easy or difficult do you find it to fix your eyes on Jesus and why?

This week how do you plan to FIX your eyes on Jesus?

Meditate on the following verse this week. Sticking it up somewhere you can see it will help: *Psalm 36:7-9 "How priceless is your unfailing love, O God! People take refuge in the shadow of your wings. They feast on the abundance of your house; you give them drink from your river of delights. For with you is the fountain of life; in your light we see light."*

Prayer: God I know that this is a journey with you. I throw myself, once again, on you, my refuge. Your love never fails me. I will not give up but continue to run this race through to the finish line. I will come and drink and be refreshed at your fountain, and receive life. Perfect my faith Jesus. Set in me a tenacity to overcome, to throw off everything that hinders me and run. God I will diligently seek you and keep my focus on you. Make me aware of Heaven as I continue on my journey.

Growth: Your baby may weigh about two pounds now (average is 1.7 pound, 760gm) and is 14 inches (35.6cm) in length. To support the foetuses' growing body, the spine is getting stronger and more supple. The spine, though no longer than the span of the average adult hand, it is now made up of 150 joints, 33 rings, and some 1,000 ligaments. Air sacs in the lungs form now, the lungs begin to secrete a greasy substance called surfactant. Without surfactant the foetal lungs would stick together and couldn't expand after the baby is born. Your baby's eyes are opening and beginning to blink this week and the retinas begin to form. Brain wave activity for hearing, touch and sight begins to be detectable.

✦

Week 27 - **Thoughts**

> *Psalm 16:9 Therefore my heart is glad and my tongue rejoices; my body also will rest secure.*

> *2 Corinthians 10:5 We demolish arguments and every pretension that sets itself up against the knowledge of God, and we take captive every thought to make it obedient to Christ.*

> *Proverbs 18:20-21 From the fruit of their mouth a person's stomach is filled; with the harvest of their lips they are satisfied. The tongue has the power of life and death, and those who love it will eat its fruit.*

> *1 Corinthians 2:16 "Who has known the mind of the Lord so as to instruct him?" But we have the mind of Christ.*

This is what I find myself thinking of often in regard to my birth:

....

....

....

....

This is what I think of when I think of being a Mum:

....

....

....

....

This is what I think when people are negative towards me:

....
....
....
....

Thinking of the following three things makes me happy and boosts my faith:

1:

2:

3:

In 'Week 7 Hearing Gods plan', you may have written down some things that came to mind that were negative about your pregnancy, birth or baby. Refer to this previous list from Week 7 and see if it still applies. You may find, that in the journey of faith you have had in the last few weeks that you are not thinking the same thoughts. Write below your comments on your list from Week 7 and your thoughts now:

....
....
....
....

Your heart is the place where this all gets worked out. Examine your heart. We often push down thoughts and think that by ignoring them, they do not have power over us. Be truthful with yourself. What thoughts are running in your mind, perhaps only in the background? If negative thoughts are there then they need to be dealt with. If they are not dealt with then you will not reach your potential in childbirth. You can only lie to yourself and it is only you who will miss out. *(Proverbs 17:20 One whose heart is corrupt does not prosper; one whose tongue is perverse falls into trouble.)* Below, write down the things that are currently running through your mind. They may be the same as in Week 7, or you may have a completely different list.

Do a scripture study on the corresponding truth to the negative thought you are entertaining:

Negative thought   *Truth*

- Example: I will have a long labour

Exodus 1:19 I am a woman of the covenant, I will give birth quickly.

-

-

-

-

-

-

-

-

-

-

Prayer: Jesus I lay all these negative thoughts at your feet. I know that you paid the price for all negativity. I choose to believe your truth. I take every thought and make it captive to the truth that supersedes it.

Go through the list of negative thoughts you believe and renounce them one by one. i.e: I renounce the lie that I will have a long drawn-out labour. I break all agreement I have made with this lie. I choose to believe that I am a woman of the covenant. I am strong and lively and will give birth quickly.

> *Isaiah 38:1-7 In those days Hezekiah became ill and was at the point of death. The prophet Isaiah son of Amoz went to him and said, "This is what the LORD says: Put your house in order, because you are going to die; you will not recover." Hezekiah turned his face to the wall and prayed to the LORD, "Remember, LORD, how I have walked before you faithfully and with wholehearted devotion and have done what is good in your eyes." And Hezekiah wept bitterly. Then the word of the LORD came to Isaiah: "Go and tell Hezekiah, 'This is what the LORD, the God of your father David, says: I have heard your prayer and seen your tears; I will add fifteen years to your life. And I will deliver you and this city from the hand of the king of Assyria. I will defend this city. This is the LORD's sign to you that the LORD will do what he has promised.*

Even if a negative thing is to take place in the future, if you think it or someone else prophecies it over you, it is not the end. Prayer is a powerful weapon. Do not ignore a 'nudge' in the spirit. Even if it is negative, God may be showing you your current trajectory. It does NOT mean that you have to maintain the course you are on. Do not give up or get depressed. It's the Spirit saying... "this is the way, walk in it. At the moment you are two steps to the right of *the way*." Prayer changes the outcome of our current course or trajectory.

Write below those negative things that you believe God may have warned you of. Or that you simply cannot shift from your thinking. Also note down the negative things that medical staff may have said to you:

1:

2:

3:

4:

Take each point and pray into it. Ask the Lord what He meant. Ask why you can't shift the thought. Ask if it is simply fear that needs to be dealt with in your heart, or if there is truth to the thought. Pray into why doctors have said certain things to you. Come boldly before His throne and speak with God with faith. For example, if you think you will have a caesarian, ask what is happening in your body that would lead you to that outcome, then pray into it. If you think it's because the baby is the wrong way than speak over your baby for him/her to move. Pray and expect your prayer to change your outcome. Write below what God says to you:

....
....
....
....
....
....
....
....
....
....
....
....
....
....
....
....
....
....
....
....
....
....
....
....
....
....

Growth: Toward the end of the seventh month, the network of nerves to the ear is complete. Your baby's hearing continues to develop, they start to recognise your voice as well as your partner's. Your baby will grow over an inch this week. Average size is now 14.4 inches (36.6cm) and 1.9 pound (875gm).

Third Trimester

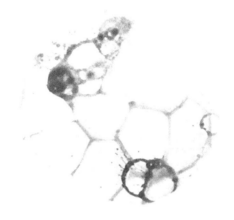

Weeks Twenty Seven - Forty Plus

Picture of bump!

Around the largest part of my belly I measure:

When I see this picture I feel:

(Space for a picture of your bump)

Week 28 - **Covered**

When I think about my baby inside me I feel:

When my baby moves I feel:

> *Psalm 91:4 He will cover you with His feathers, and under His wings you will find refuge; His faithfulness will be your shield and rampart.*

What thoughts come to mind when you read Psalm 91:4?:

....

....

....

Spend time with God and let Him show you things in your home that are not under His covering. He may show you things that you have let take His place. He may show you areas of your life that you do not trust Him with. *Joshua 24:15, But as for me and my household, we will serve the LORD.* He may show you areas where your house does not serve Him. List below what He reveals to you:

....

....

....

....

....

....

....

Prayer: God, I will be my baby's covering. I choose to take a position of intercession. I will pray and declare on my child's behalf, until they are old enough to do so themselves. I will cover them with your presence while they are inside of me. I will choose to put them first, and take care of what atmosphere I surround them with. I will be joyful so that my baby will feel loved. I will be peaceful so that my baby will be at rest. I will eat well so that my baby is healthy. I will contend in prayer, even now, for them to know you from an early age. I will pray for their character, their emotions, their friends, their schooling, their job and their future partner. God reveal yourself to me more fully, as I press into you, so that my children may have the best starting point possible. Jesus I will set my house right, I will live holy and pleasing to you, I will create a heavenly atmosphere in my home for my baby to grow up in.

After reading this prayer how do you feel?

Are there any things that you need to change before your baby comes?

How do you intend to put your house in order?

> *Proverbs 22:6 Start children off on the way they should go, and even when they are old they will not turn from it.*

Imagine a moment - what kind of adult your baby will turn into? Write a list of qualities you think are important for them to have:

....

....

Thinking of those qualities, how will you start your child on the path to becoming an adult with those characteristics?

....

....

....

....

....

....

....

Are these qualities you have yourself?

Are there any things you need to change, in order for you to nurture your child, into the adult you envision them becoming?

When the Word says we are to train a child in the way they should go, it is not simply talking about training them to have great values and a moral standing. It is not even necessarily talking about starting your child off on the Christian path in order that they will become adult Christians! It is referring to training each individual child in the particular way *they* should go. Each person has a unique gifting and call on them from birth, as a parent we are to prepare our child for adulthood within the call and gifts that we see and that God tells us are in them. We are to cover our children with a secure environment to make mistakes as they head towards the outworking of this call.

We will normally have a different call on ourselves than that of the call on our kids, so we are not to cover them with the boundaries that would help us, as our boundaries may end up restraining them. For example, if a child has a call of a pioneer upon them, they are gifted with risk taking and obscure thinking, but the mother of this child has a peaceful gift and a quiet spirit, she is dependable and faithful, she has been called to settle in one place and make a safe environment for people to come into. This mother will try and teach their boisterous, 'difficult' child to be calmer, to sit still in story time, to complete a task, and they will discipline so that their child fits within the status quo.

With this gift mix in one house you can imagine if the gifting on the child as a pioneer is unknown to the parents, when this child is a teenager the unsettledness that is a gift to the child's call will, without grooming and understanding, become a rebellious spirit that reaps chaos and unrest in family and school life. However if the parents are shrewd enough to inquire of the Lord the child's abilities and call, they can teach the child how to be at rest within themselves, while having the ability to think outside the box, how to finish a task rather than dash onto the next thing.

The family will be less frustrated because they understand which tasks to give to this energetic leader and not expect long attention spans for 'mundane' things.

Circle the words that sound most like you and then underline all the words that least describe you:

Organised Structured Fun Quiet Adventurous Random Funny Sensitive Rude Fast-passed Calm Angry Shy Boisterous Peaceful Energetic Talkative Proper Headstrong Withdrawn Honest Friendly Loyal Perfectionist Drastic Dramatic Internalised Loud Screamer Tearful Outgoing Harsh Calculated Chameleon Open Obliging Wise Mature Indignant Loveable Movable Punctual Brave Playful Wilful

If your child ends up having traits like the characteristics you have underlined, how will that challenge you?

In what ways would you work with their characteristics?

Think of ways that you would go about parenting a child that is so different from you:

Jesus in what areas will my baby's father and I differ in thought and gift from our child?

....
....
....

How should we manage this?

Are there any activities, hobbies or classes that would benefit our child?

With my baby's call in mind, what can I do to aid them to make the decision to serve you Jesus?

....
....
....
....
....
....
....
....
....
....
....
....
....
....
....
....
....
....
....
....

Prayer: God, make me into a wise woman. May I see my child the way that you do. Help me God to parent them, in the knowledge of their destiny. I pray that I may cover them as you cover me. God cover my shortcomings and be faithful to me. Help me to see through the things that I will find a challenge in the personality of my child, help me to train them in the way *they* should go. Teach me Holy Spirit to be the perfect mother for this particular child.

Growth: Eyebrows and eyelashes are now very noticeable. Hair on baby's head is growing longer. Eyes are completely formed now. Your baby's body is getting plump and rounded. Most of that increase is muscle tissue and bone. Fat will be added during the third trimester. Muscle tone is improving. Your baby weighs in now at 2.2 pounds (1005gm) and is 14.8 inches (37.6cm).

✦

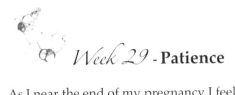 *Week 29* - **Patience**

As I near the end of my pregnancy I feel:

I am / am not becoming anxious because:

I am usually a fairly anxious / non anxious person because:

I get impatient when I think about:

> *James 5:7 Be patient, then, brothers and sisters, until the Lord's coming. See how the farmer waits for the land to yield its valuable crop, patiently waiting for the autumn and spring rains.*

Think for a moment about the agricultural cycle, how everything has a season and an order to which it is confined. Now think about your baby developing inside you. Think about the process your baby has gone through from the first moment of conception until now. It may feel like you have been pregnant for a while, but in twenty nine weeks your baby has grown tremendously. However, they still have a way to go before being able to sustain life on their own. Your baby is developing to perfection and they need time to finish that process, time on baby's behalf and patience on yours!

"Patience is the capacity to accept or tolerate delay, trouble, or suffering without getting angry or upset" *(Dictionary)*. Patience for me conjures up a sense of serenity. No matter the circumstances, you wait with dignity and grace. It is by the Holy Spirit's empowering that we receive the capacity to be patient. *Colossians 1:10-12, So that you may live a life worthy of the Lord and please Him in every way: bearing fruit in every good work, growing in the knowledge of God, being strengthened with all power according to His glorious might so that you may have great endurance and patience, and giving joyful thanks to the Father, who has qualified you to share in the inheritance of His holy people in the kingdom of light.*

Spend a few moments with Holy Spirit. He is already with you and has already empowered you, given you the patience you need even if you are not aware of it. Talk to Him and ask for Him to make you aware of His empowerment. You could close your eyes and ask Him what that empowerment looks like on you.

Reflect on how you feel now you have done that:

....
....
....
....
....

Hebrews 6:12 We do not want you to become lazy, but to imitate those who through faith and patience inherit what has been promised.

Patience is not sitting still, doing nothing, waiting for the end to come. Faith and patience go together. Faith is impotent without deeds *(James 2:26).* We are not to become lazy in our patience but to connect faith to patience. We become serenely expectant of the outcome. We are not grabbing for the end result, jostling and making it happen, but we are quietly assured that what we are believing for will happen, in the appropriate season of our ninth month.

In one sentence write the outcome you are expecting for your labour:

....
....
....

Circle below the sentence that best describes your current state of mind:

1:      *Lazy, waiting for the outcome I want to fall into my lap!*

2:      *Occasionally thinking about the outcome and praying it over from time to time.*

3:      *Serenely expectant, confident, in constant relationship with God.*

4:      *Expectant for what I am believing for with moments of doubt.*

5:      *Fervently going after the end goal, I can't wait until it's arrived!*

6:      *Wanting to have the expected outcome, but wanting pregnancy to be over now.*

7:      *Calm; wishing for the outcome but not convinced I will receive it in full.*

8:      *Sudden shifts in emotion from calm to anxious.*

How do you feel about where you are at?

Is there anywhere on the list that you would rather say to be true?

Is there anything that you feel you need to do to improve your balance of patience and faith?

Jesus, what do I need to do to have a correct faith - patience balance?

What makes you impatient in everyday life?

Can you think of any area of your life that you can practice patience, so that this fruit of the Spirit has a chance to be exercised and grown in you?

Jesus what makes me anxious for my expected labour outcome?

....
....
....
....

Jesus, I give you my fear. What has opened this area of fear?

Jesus, do I need to forgive anyone for opening this area or fear up to me?

Do you need to hand over past disappointing experiences to God? You may need to forgive yourself for not obtaining the outcome you set for yourself. You may need to forgive God if you feel like He wasn't faithful to you. Take time to process this with God.

....
....
....
....
....
....

Hebrews 6:12 says that we also need to imitate those who have gone before us. Name below some people who you look at, as those who walk a life of faith, and give reasons why:

....
....
....
....

In what ways can you imitate them?

....
....
....

Prayer: Lord I give you all my unrest. I lay all anxiety at your feet. I am so excited to meet my child. I give you thanks Father God. I will share in your inheritance. Holy Spirit help me to walk in your fruit; patience. Help me to grow in the knowledge of you so that I may be strengthened and ready. I will live in your peace. Help me to endure patiently to the end. Mind, you will not become anxious. God help me address the balance of faith and patience in my journey through pregnancy. Help me remain calmly expectant, so I can receive everything that you have promised me.

Say out loud: *"Holy Spirit make it possible for me to experience your patience."* Take a deep breath and exhale your anxiousness to Him. Think of Him, leading you beside quiet waters. This week aim to spend five minutes every day, just breathing out your impatience and waiting for the Spirit of patience to rest upon you.

Growth: Fat continues to accumulate under the skin. Your baby's brain can control primitive breathing and body temperatures. Your baby is also moving from side to side, but is probably still upright. In the next few weeks, your baby will move to the head down birthing position. Baby's length is now approximately 15.2 inches (38.6cm) and weight is 2.54 pounds (1153gm).

Extra reading: Job 33:4, Ezekiel Psalm 150:6, 37:5-10, John 20:22.

 *Week 30* - **Abide**

What does the word 'abide' mean to you?

....
....
....

This week spend three times each day sitting and resting in Him. Schedule in the time or make it the same time each day (ie: before breakfast, during lunch and before bed). At the end of the week note below the difference it has made to you in doing this:

....
....
....
....
....
....
....

Read the following Scriptures out loud over yourself five times. Repeat this declaration of scripture over yourself this week as often as you can.

Psalm 62:1-2 Truly my soul finds rest in God; my salvation comes from Him. Truly He is my rock and my salvation; He is my fortress, I will never be shaken.

Psalm 91:1-3 Whoever dwells in the shelter of the Most High will rest in the shadow of the Almighty. I will say of the LORD, "He is my refuge and my fortress, my God, in whom I trust." Surely He will save you from the fowler's snare and from the deadly pestilence.

John 15:7 If you abide in Me, and My words abide in you, you will ask what you desire, and it shall be done for you.

> *Hebrew 4:9-11 There remains, then, a Sabbath-rest for the people of God; for anyone who enters God's rest also rests from their works, just as God did from His. Let us, therefore, make every effort to enter that rest, so that no one will perish by following their example of disobedience.*

On a scale of 1-10 how easy do you find it to rest:

Physically:

And in your thought life:

Give reasons as to why you have given yourself the above scores:

....
....
....
....
....

This week pick a song that you can play and rest in God's presence to. What is the song and why have you chosen it?

This week plan to do three activities that you find relaxing. List below what they are and when you intend to do them:

1:

2:

3:

List three ways that you can abide in Him this week:

1:

2:

3:

Prayer: God help me to develop a lifestyle of abiding in you. Make me a lover of your word. I will actively make your word abide in me as I take refuge in your presence. I make a decision to spend time just being with you this week. I will rest and know that I do not need to strive to achieve my goals, but trust you as my refuge and my fortress.

Growth: Your baby is nearly three pounds now and spends more and more time practising opening and closing their eyelids. The eyes can move from side to side, following a light source. Baby may even reach out to touch the light. Toenails are reaching their final growth stage. Bone marrow is now in charge of red blood cell production. Red blood cells transport oxygen and remove waste such as carbon monoxide and other gases. Even within the womb your baby is capable of producing tears. By the end of this week, your baby is 15.7 inches (39.9cm) long and weighs 2.91 pounds (1319gm).

Extra reading: Psalm 116:8, Psalm 119:136, Isaiah 25:8, Luke 7:38.

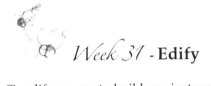

Week 31 - **Edify**

To edify means to build up, instruct and improve. Edification strengthens us. The Bible tells us that joy is our strength. We must go into His presence where we find fullness of joy, be strengthened and built up. Edified: To edify ourselves also means to be instructed. The Bible is our source of instruction. When we meditate on The Word and who He is, we edify ourselves - we are improved! When we know God we do great exploits (Daniel 11:32, NKJ). When we know Him through His words and do as He says, we are prosperous and successful.

> *Joshua 1:8 Do not let this Book of the Law depart from your mouth; meditate on it day and night, so that you may be careful to do everything written in it. Then you will be prosperous and successful.*

What does a 'prosperous and successful' childbirth look like to you?

....
....
....
....
....
....
....

How much does having a 'supernatural childbirth' mean to you on the scale of 1-10?

To be successful then we need to pursue Him, His word and edify ourselves.

In what ways will you pursue Him this week?

In what ways can you meditate on The Word day and night?

I believe that knowing Him is the key to everything. How well do you feel your relationship with God is doing? Explain your relationship with Him:

....
....
....
....

Think about God and His individual characteristics within the Trinity. What kind of relationship do you have with each member of the Godhead? Can you approach Father, jump up on His lap and snuggle into your heavenly Daddy? Is Jesus your best friend? Do you confide in Him and share your secrets with Him? Do you play with Him and have a fun relationship together, like you would a best friend or brother? Is Holy Spirit real to you? Do you sense His presence and communicate with Him? Is He your comforter, your teacher?

How can you improve these individual relationships?

Which of the Godhead do you have the most relationship with? Why do you think that is?

....
....

Which relationship do you think needs the most improvement and why?

....
....

Spend time with God now and ask Him to reveal Himself to you in a new way. If you find this a challenge, set a timer for ten minutes. Read a Bible verse that you find encouraging; perhaps a Psalm. Relax and wait for His presence to come. Talk to Him and wait for Him to answer. Write below what you saw, felt, sensed or heard. There is no wrong answer:

....
....
....
....

Encouragement always builds us up and therefore we also feel edified when we understand what God thinks about us. Spend a moment and ask each of the Godhead what they think about you, or how they see you. Anything encouraging and positive that comes to mind is ok. You may get a mental image, or feel an emotion like peace or love. Write below what you saw, sensed or heard from each member of the Godhead:

Father God:

Jesus:

Holy Spirit:

If you are struggling use *Psalm 77:11-13 "I will remember the deeds of the LORD; yes, I will remember your miracles of long ago. I will consider all your works and meditate on all your mighty deeds. Your ways, God, are holy. What god is as great as our God?"* Think about all God has done in the past for you personally. Spend time with Him again and start by thanking Him for all you remember. You can also find a Bible story that inspires you and read about how good God is. You will find that when you have finished reading or speaking out your thanks to God, that your spirit is edified. *Psalm 1:1-3 Blessed is the one who does not walk in step with the wicked or stand in the way that sinners take or sit in the company of mockers, but whose delight is in the law of the LORD, and who meditates on His law day and night. That person is like a tree planted by streams of water, which yields its fruit in season and whose leaf does not wither— whatever they do prospers.* When we read The Word of God, (or 'the law' as it is referred to in this passage) we become strong and healthy and so do our babies.

Just as there are ways to edify ourselves, there are things that have the opposite effect. *Psalm 119:44-45 I will always obey your law, forever and ever. I will walk about in freedom, for I have sought out your precepts.* As we search out The Word of God and obey what we see in it, it brings us freedom. We improve, moving from bondage to freedom as we read and digest The Word. And by improving we edify ourselves.

Spend two minutes and ask God if there is anything that you do, or align yourself with, that does not edify you. Write below what He tells you and what you intend to do about them:

....
....
....
....
....
....

The most effective way to edify yourself is to spend time each day praying in tongues (*1 Corinthians 14:4 Anyone who speaks in a tongue edifies themselves*). As the spirit prays through you, He utters things on your behalf and prays exactly what you need over your current situation. As you speak, your spiritual core is strengthened. Set yourself a challenge to pray in tongues for five minutes, every hour of everyday this week and note here how that has impacted you:

....
....
....

....
....
....
....
....
....
....
....
....
....
....
....

If you've never spoken in tongues before and you would like to start moving in this gift from Holy Spirit; simply start to thank God for the gift that you already have, ask Holy Spirit to come and immerse you in Himself and start to say the first words that come to you. It may sound silly at first but as you set aside any embarrassment you will quickly start to grow in the gift and feel its benefits.

Prayer: God I choose to obey your law, your Word. I will seek your Word so that it becomes active in my life. Teach me your ways God so that I become strong in you. So that I become free. I will delight in your Word, I will not wither, but I will prosper. I will yield my fruit, my baby, in season. Make me a lover of your Word. I will edify myself in you.

> **Growth:** The rate of physical growth slows down a little, your baby won't get much longer now but will gain a lot of weight during the rest of your pregnancy. Bones are growing and hardening as calcium, phosphorus and iron are being stored. Your baby is 16.2 inches (41.1cm) long and weighs 3.3 pounds (1502gm). Their brain enters another period of rapid growth, producing hundreds of billions of new nerve cells. Lungs are the only major organ left to complete development.

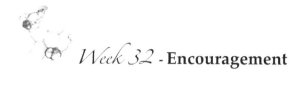

Week 32 - **Encouragement**

> *2 Thessalonians 2:16-17 May our Lord Jesus Christ himself and God our Father, who loved us and by His grace gave us eternal encouragement and good hope, encourage your hearts and strengthen you in every good deed and word.*

> *Psalm 103:1-5 Praise the LORD, my soul; all my inmost being, praise his holy name. Praise the LORD, my soul, and forget not all His benefits—who forgives all your sins and heals all your diseases, who redeems your life from the pit and crowns you with love and compassion, who satisfies your desires with good things so that your youth is renewed like the eagle's.*

Use the words of these scriptures from Thessalonians and Psalms. Put them into your own words and make them your prayer. Confess it out loud to God and over your body and soul. Insert your name where appropriate. Write out your prayer then pray it each day this week:

....
....
....
....
....
....
....
....
....
....
....
....

> *1 Samuel 30:6 David was greatly distressed, for the men spoke of stoning him because the souls of them all were bitterly grieved, each man for his sons and daughters. But David encouraged and strengthened himself in the Lord his God.*

In the midst of an awful situation David was able to overcome his discouragement and encouraged himself in the Lord. He had a covenant with God and he drew on the benefits of that covenant. To overcome discouragement we need to focus on the One who has the solution. It is only in His presence that we can feel encouraged. In His presence is fullness of joy (Psalm 16:11). In an atmosphere of joy it is difficult to be discouraged. Remind yourself what He has done for you and who He is. Through Christ you have the same and even greater covenant than King David. You too can draw from its benefits. Read the story of King David in 1 Samuel to see how bad his situation was and how he was still able to pull himself out of it.

Reflect on what God has done for you so far:

....
....
....
....
....
....
....
....
....
....
....
....

A good way to encourage yourself is to write out all the good things that have been spoken over you; any prophecy that you have had; words that you have been given, and things that the Lord has told you about your future. You can even record them and listen back to them on a regular basis. Schedule in time this week to make a list, or start a notebook of all that has been spoken over you. Write out five of your favourite things:

1:

2:

3:

4:

5:

> *Matthew 10:27 What I tell you in the dark, speak in the daylight; what is whispered in your ear, proclaim from the roofs.*

Start to change your language this week, see if you can catch yourself out. Do your words speak encouragement over yourself and your situation?

List a few other ways that you can encourage yourself this week:

....

....

....

Prayer: God thank you for giving me eternal encouragement. Encourage my heart. I rely on your love, saturate me. Strengthen me in my walk through childbearing. Renew me so that I can fly like an eagle and sore above my circumstances. Remind me of all that you have already done for me.

Growth: Your baby is 3.75 pounds (1702gm) now and is 16.7 inches (42.4cm) long. Your baby has less room to move around now. All five senses are working. Around the eighth month babies have periods of dream sleep (REM).

Extra reading: Sleep and dreaming; Psalm 121:4, Proverbs 3:24, Psalm 126:1, Joel 2:28

✦

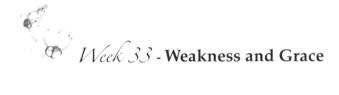 *Week 33* **- Weakness and Grace**

> *2 Corinthians 12:9-10 But He said to me, "My grace is sufficient for you, for my power is made perfect in weakness." Therefore I will boast all the more gladly about my weaknesses, so that Christ's power may rest on me. That is why, for Christ's sake, I delight in weaknesses, in insults, in hardships, in persecutions, in difficulties. For when I am weak, then I am strong.*

In what areas have you recently been experiencing weaknesses, insults, hardships, persecutions, or difficulties?

....
....
....
....
....
....

Enquire of the Lord as to how you can boast in these areas of difficulty:

....
....
....
....
....
....

We need to be self aware and recognise in which areas our personal weaknesses lay. We need not strive to become strong in these areas, but press ourselves into His grace. Grace is His strengthening: its enabling. When we know where we are weak we can press into His strength in those areas. When we press into His grace, into who He is, we see Him. As we see Him, we become like Him; and are therefore being made strong. It is not striving for ourselves to be strong, but a complete reliance in His great strength.

List at least five ways that you are weak:

i.e: I am not very compassionate

1:

2:

3:

4:

5:

Search the Bible to find how He is strong in the areas you are weak.

List them below:

i.e. He crowns me with love and compassion - Psalm 103:4

1:

2:

3:

4:

5:

Imagine yourself as strong in your areas of weakness.

Describe what strength would look like:

1:

2:

3:

4:

5:

List, at least five areas, things, or characteristics where you see yourself as strong:

1:

2:

3:

4:

5:

Ask three friends to tell you three strengths they see in you and fill in the table with their responses.

Name	1st strength	2nd strength	3rd strength

> Zechariah 12:8-9 On that day the LORD will shield those who live in Jerusalem, so that the feeblest among them will be like David, and the house of David will be like God, like the angel of the LORD going before them. On that day I will set out to destroy all the nations that attack Jerusalem.

God is our shield. Even if in some areas we feel feeble and weak, God makes us like King David. David was a man after God's own heart, he endured to the end and is one of the great fathers of the faith. So in our weakness we are made into a woman of faith with a heart after God, strong enough to defeat a giant and be king of a nation. Now in the areas we are strong God makes us even stronger: He makes us as strong as Himself. God enables us to be strong, even if we are already strong, He pushes us to excel using His supernatural enabling, by grace going past our own strength.

How do you feel after reading the verses in Zechariah?

Grace is the *free and unmerited favour of God manifest in salvation and the bestowal of blessings (Dictionary)*. We do nothing to deserve grace, grace is given as a free gift, it is His *courteous goodwill* towards us.

God is wanting you to succeed, how does knowing that affect your outlook?

....

....

Prayer: I know my weaknesses; but I also know that you are strong. Your grace is more than enough to see me through. You are my shield and even if I am weak you make me as strong as David! You are my protector and will destroy all that stands against me. I rest in the goodness of your grace. I draw on your grace and ask for more of your supernatural enabling, I know that you have all that I need to be strong. Where I am already strong you come and stand behind me to make me immovable!

Growth: If your baby is a boy, his testicles will be descending from his abdomen into his scrotum. Sometimes one or both testicles won't move into position until after birth. Your infant is now 17.2 inches (43.7cm) long and weighs 4.23 pounds (1918gm).

✦

 *Week 34* - **Faithfulness**

> *Psalm 91:4 He will cover you with His feathers, and under His wings you will find refuge; His faithfulness will be your shield and rampart.*

Write a few ways in which during your pregnancy, you have felt shielded by God:

1:

2:

3:

> *2 Timothy 2:11-13 "Here is a trustworthy saying: If we died with Him, we will also live with Him; if we endure, we will also reign with Him. If we disown Him, He will also disown us; if we are faithless, He remains faithful, for He cannot disown himself."*

You do not need to do anything and God will still prove faithful to you. God's nature is faithfulness, therefore if He was not faithful, He would disown His very self. Find refuge under the shadow of His wing for He is your faithful shield. The dictionary definition of *'faithful'* is *"loyal, constant and steadfast."*

When you think of God's faithfulness how do you feel?:

> *Isaiah 38:19 The living, the living—they praise you, as I am doing today; parents tell their children about your faithfulness.*

Think of three times where God has proven Himself faithful to you throughout your life, speak to your bump out loud and tell your baby what God has done. Also write them down below:

1:

2:

3:

Now think about your pregnancy so far and write three ways He has been faithful:

1:

2:

3:

Spend a few minutes thanking God for His amazing faithfulness. Let your heart overflow with gratitude as you ponder on what He has already done. As you do, you will not be able to stop praise springing forth. Praise then makes your heart glad and this has a direct influence on how your body reacts.

Are there things that are threatening to consume you?

Write down the things that you are still grappling with:

....
....
....
....

> *Lamentations 3:22-24 Because of the LORD's great love we are not consumed, for His compassions never fail. They are new every morning; great is your faithfulness. I say to myself, "The LORD is my portion; therefore I will wait for Him."*

Close your eyes. Take a deep breath and let Him take your worry and strife. Say out loud to yourself: *"The LORD is my portion; therefore I will wait for him."* Breath in again. Repeat this verse in Lamentations as many times as you need to until you believe it.

Each morning this week repeat the verse and wait for God's compassion to come upon you, Lamentations promises that He will never fail us.

> *Hebrew 3:6 But Christ is faithful as the Son over God's house. And we are His house, if indeed we hold firmly to our confidence and the hope in which we glory.*

Remind yourself what you are in hope for by writing below. What are you sure and certain of for the remainder of your pregnancy, and for your labour:

1:

2:

3:

4:

5:

Prayer: Jesus you are over me, you cover me, and I rest under your almighty, powerful wings. I know you to be faithful, I have seen your faithfulness at work in the past and I will see it again now. I will not be consumed. I will do my part and hold firmly to what I hope for. But even if it appears as though I do this all 'wrong', you can't help but be faithful to me. I do not need to impress you. I do not need to prove anything. You are faithful by nature. Your faithfulness is my shield. I feel safe in the fact that you will prove yourself faithful once again in my time of need. For your glory, I will have a testimony. I know that I cannot do this alone, I cling to your faithfulness. In my weakness you are strong.

Quiet your heart then ask God the following question and listen for His gentle answer. "God I ask you to show me any area where I do not believe that you are faithful":

....

....

....
....

If anything comes to mind then lift up your disappointment and lack of trust to Him. Then ask if there is anyone who you need to forgive, and forgive who comes to mind, including God himself. (I am not saying that God has ever done anything untrustworthy, however our hearts often feel owed by people, even God, when they don't react or respond in the way we would have had them do. As we choose to forgive, we open the door to the healing of our hearts.) Now ask God to reveal to you why He is trustworthy.

Write below what He tells you:

....
....
....
....
....
....
....
....
....
....

Growth: Your baby is exactly like a newborn now. Eyes are open when awake and closed when asleep. And you may be able to feel the sleeping routine your baby is in. Antibodies from your blood are being transferred to their body. These immunities continue to build until birth then breast milk will add even more protection against disease. Your baby may have already turned to a head-down position in preparation for birth. If this is your first baby, your baby may be settling into the pelvis with their head pressing against your cervix. Your little one's length is 17.7 inches (45cm) and weight is 4.7 pounds (2146 g).

 # *Week 35* - **Testimony**

Testimonies are an invitation. Testimonies lift our expectation. Faith rises and you have an opportunity to experience the same thing. Testimonies have the power to reproduce themselves in your life, if you are willing to take hold of them and make them your own.

> *Psalm 126:1-3 When the LORD restored the fortunes of Zion, we were like those who dreamed. Our mouths were filled with laughter, our tongues with songs of joy. Then it was said among the nations, "The LORD has done great things for them." The LORD has done great things for us, and we are filled with joy.*

Allow yourself to dream, it can be yours or you can take someone else's fulfilled dream - their testimony. When someone else's victory is restored, by getting healed or experiencing Gods provision, we can then claim that dream for ourselves.

We can triumph over the enemy because of what Jesus did on the cross, but also by testimony. *Revelation 12:11 They triumphed over him by the blood of the Lamb and by the word of their testimony.* When we recall what Jesus has already done for us and when we make the testimonies of others our own by believing in them, we triumph. God is not a respecter of persons, therefore when you hear of what God has done in the life of another person, by His grace, compassion and faithfulness we can have the same thing replicated in our lives.

> *Psalm 77:11-13 I will remember the deeds of the LORD; yes, I will remember your miracles of long ago. I will consider all your works and meditate on all your mighty deeds." Your ways, God, are holy. What god is as great as our God?*

Do a study of women who have gone before you and seen the Lord do great things for them in childbirth. Find Biblical accounts of pregnancy and childbirth. Go back and re-read the first three chapters of Pregnancy in His Presence, along with the last testimonies chapter, then find other resources that have women's testimonies in them. Talk to all the Christian mothers you know and ask them how God was faithful to them in childbirth. (You can ask them to leave out any negative bits! Get them to concentrate on what God did do).

Write below who you asked and what you found out:

....
....
....
....
....
....
....
....

Write below what encouraged you the most from hearing or reading these stories:

....
....
....
....
....
....
....

Psalm 103:1-5 Praise the LORD, my soul; all my inmost being, praise His holy name. Praise the LORD, my soul, and forget not all His benefits—who forgives all your sins and heals all your diseases, who redeems your life from the pit and crowns you with love and compassion, who satisfies your desires with good things so that your youth is renewed like the eagle's.

Spend a few moments letting praise rise in you for what the Lord is capable of. Thank Him for all the specifics. You can go through them one by one. Remember, *'forget none of His benefits'*. As you remember the great things He has done let joy rise up inside of you. Joy is your strength.

Recalling testimonies is a great way to grow in strength, because when we read good and positive things we get happy!

Note here how you now feel: (i.e: Do you feel strengthened from reading?)

....
....
....

Each day this week search the internet for healing testimonies of God and search the Bible for 'impossible' miracles that took place. Encourage yourself through what God has done. It can become addictive! You can feel your faith begin to rise as you see God's heart for people all over the world. Write into the table what you found out:

Day	Scripture reference/ Testimony title	Overview	Why you chose this one
1			
2			
3			
4			

Day	Scripture reference/ Testimony title	Overview	Why you chose this one
5			
6			
7			

Prayer: Jesus help me to recall all that you have done for me. I will not forget! I will praise you this week and let my mind focus on you, the author and perfecter of my faith. Holy Spirit help praise to bubble up inside of me. Remind me of all your exploits. Let faith arise a fresh inside of me. God increase my capacity for understanding how unconstrained you are. Let my life be a testimony of your greatness and faithfulness.

Growth: The average baby weighs almost five and a half pounds now. Fat accumulates and plumps up the limbs this week. These fat layers help to regulate baby's body temperature. Hearing is fully developed. Your baby is 18.2 inches (46.2cm) long and weighs 5.3 pounds (2383gm). The testes have completed their descent in baby boys.

✦

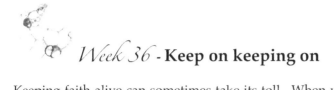

Week 36 - **Keep on keeping on**

Keeping faith alive can sometimes take its toll. When you live day in day out in hope of what is to come, you can often feel like it's never going to come, or your resolve for what you're hoping for begins to waiver. *Ephesians 6:13 Therefore put on the full armour of God, so that when the day of evil comes, you may be able to stand your ground, and after you have done everything, to stand.* You may get to a point, perhaps you have reached it, where you have done everything. You have prayed, read, hoped, believed, talked, confessed, worshipped, prayed some more and repeated the whole process over and over again on a daily basis. You really have nothing else to do. You are full of the knowledge of what you have to do practically, you are prayed up and spiritually ready, you know you are in faith, you are at peace. This is exactly the moment when you feel like you can take a break! Do not misunderstand: daily rest is good and right. However, faith should never take a day off! I am not asking you to strive; if you have to strive to work up faith, then you are not truly in faith. What I want to encourage you to do is to STAY in faith. You are doing a great job - you're almost there. Even if you have no one in your life cheering you on I am cheering for you, the great cloud of witnesses are cheering you on, God is cheering over you. You can do it just a little bit longer. Keep on standing. God wants you to succeed, He's made you more than a conqueror and it's all because of His love for you. And for those areas that you know you are not in faith for, He is faithful; He has your best interests at heart and He walks tenderly with you and your baby.

How prepared do you feel on the scale of 1-10?

Do you feel like you have done and are doing everything to be prepared?

Do you feel weary or ready to give up, urgently wishing for the end?

If so, how do you keep standing? Read the whole of Ephesians 6. Note what the armour of God is and how to put it on?

....

....

> *1 Corinthians 1:8-9 He will also keep you firm to the end, so that you will be blameless on the day of our Lord Jesus Christ. God is faithful, who has called you into fellowship with His Son, Jesus Christ our Lord.*

We must always remember that it is Him who is faithful and He is the one that will ultimately keep us firm to the end. When you feel like you can't keep on, He enables you to keep doing so. The key in this verse is *'fellowship'*. It is in a place of intimacy with Him that we find His strength. *Isaiah 40:31 But those who hope in the LORD will renew their strength. They will soar on wings like eagles; they will run and not grow weary, they will walk and not be faint.* It's when we see the Lord and know Him; when we really see Him and know what He is capable of; when we see even if for just a moment from the perspective of Heaven, our energy is renewed. One look at His smiling face or the sound of His cheer for us running our race spurs us on.

In what ways this week can you spend more time with Him?:

1:

2:

3:

> *Hebrews 6:11-12 We want each of you to show this same diligence to the very end, so that what you hope for may be fully realised. We do not want you to become lazy, but to imitate those who through faith and patience inherit what has been promised.*

As we show diligence to the end our hope is then realised. Are there any ways you think you are not being diligent? *'Diligent'* means, "having or showing *care* and *conscientiousness*." (Dictionary)

List three areas you think you may have become lazy or apathetic in your spiritual walk:

1:

2:

3:

How or what are you able to do to fix that?:

....

....

> *Matthew 11:12 And from the days of John the Baptist until the present time, the kingdom of heaven has endured violent assault, and violent men seize it by force [as a precious prize--a share in the heavenly kingdom is sought with most ardent zeal and intense exertion]. AMP*

To conquer means to climb a mountain successfully, to successfully overcome or take control of something. *Romans 8:37-39 No, in all these things we are more than conquerors through Him who loved us. For I am convinced that neither death nor life, neither angels nor demons, neither the present nor the future, nor any powers, neither height nor depth, nor anything else in all creation, will be able to separate us from the love of God that is in Christ Jesus our Lord.* We are more than conquerors because of His love. Because He conquered death and sin for us, we too can now live a victorious life. We can conquer the mountain in front of us. In this case, childbirth! We can climb successfully to the top because of the love of God.

How well do you feel loved by God? Explain how you experience this:

....

....

....

....

Close your eyes and wait for His presence. Ask each of the Godhead in turn to show or tell you the answers to the questions in the table. We've done this exercise before but we need to keep up our connection with Him and delve deeper into His love for us, not only to see Him for who He is, but to see ourselves in the light of heaven.

	What do you think about me?	What do I look like to you?	How much do you love me?
Father			
Jesus			
Holy Spirit			

How do you now feel loved by God?

....

....

Spend a moment and ask God if you have been believing any lies about how He loves you. When something comes to mind, ask when it was that you first believed that lie as truth. Forgive anyone who was involved in teaching the lie to you, forgive yourself for believing it and then renounce it. Each day this week read over the answers you heard from each of the Godhead then stick them up somewhere for a month so that you start to renew your mind to the truth about you that has been revealed.

Read a whole gospel, (Matthew, Mark, Luke or John) this week. Look for themes of God's love running through it. Meditate on His love and thank Him for it.

What themes of love did you see when you read?

....
....
....
....
....
....
....

Prayer: God I will do everything in my power to stand, and when I have done that, I will stand some more! God it is our relationship that keeps me firm to the end, I run into you, oh Faithful one! I will not grow weary of this race but will run with ardent zeal and intense spiritual exertion. I will look at those who have gone before and be diligent to the end. I will be MORE than a conqueror. Nothing can separate me from your love, Jesus let me be more aware of your love for me. Holy Spirit reveal your word to me as I read it this week.

Growth: If it hasn't happened already, this week your baby may drop into the birth canal. Your baby's skin is growing smooth. The kidneys are fully developed and the liver has begun processing some waste. Average size is now 18.66 inches (47.4cm) and 5.78 pounds (2622gm). Between now and birth baby will gain about an ounce a day!

 *Week 37* - **Birthing partner**

> *Ruth 1:16 But Ruth replied, "Don't urge me to leave you or to turn back from you. Where you go I will go, and where you stay I will stay. Your people will be my people and your God my God."*

When choosing a birthing partner, find someone that you are confident will be able to have the heart of Ruth, that their cry to you will be the cry Ruth made to Naomi in the verse above. They will walk with you in whatever **you** want to do, not someone who will push their preference or opinion, a steadfast friend and loyal companion. Happy to lay aside their own theology, their experience of faith, pregnancy and childbirth, and pull with you. Not to be void of opinion but willing to lay aside their own thoughts to go along with yours.

> *1 Thessalonians 5:10-11 He died for us so that, whether we are awake or asleep, we may live together with him. Therefore encourage one another and build each other up, just as in fact you are doing.*

Think about the characters of your friends and relatives. Write below five people who build you up and encourage you in everyday life.

1:

2:

3:

4:

5:

> *Exodus 17:12 When Moses' hands grew tired, they took a stone and put it under him and he sat on it. Aaron and Hur held his hands up — one on one side, one on the other — so that his hands remained steady till sunset.*

Find someone with common sense, someone who is not shy of hard work. Someone that will support you physically and mentally if you get tired. The partner you choose needs to know what you want so that they can make it happen with you. You either need to pick someone who knows you very well, or you need to find someone who has motherly instincts. They may not know you as well but they 'read' people very well. They can see when they need to "put a stone under you" or "hold up your arms." Find someone who naturally speaks life, is encouraging, has a 'can do' personality, or someone who is very nurturing.

> *Romans 15:5-6 May the God who gives endurance and encouragement give you the same attitude of mind toward each other that Christ Jesus had, so that with one mind and one voice you may glorify the God and Father of our Lord Jesus Christ.*

> *Proverbs 17:17 A friend loves at all times, and is born, as is a brother, for adversity. AMP*

Find someone who will stand with you and be able to give you good advice spiritually, but also, if things don't go to plan, someone who will remain loving and adaptable. They probably need to be a pragmatic person who is not highly emotional. This personality type will be able to see the situation objectively. They will be able to keep in mind what your birthing plan is but will be able to roll with the rhythm of the situation. Look for someone who calms you but who can speak their mind without you automatically rejecting their opinion. Look for someone you trust.

List three people you trust, and explain why you trust them:

1.

2.

3.

Use the following prayer and spend time with God before you choose the right partner. It may be that your husband is very supportive and knows you better than anyone else. However you may need to ask two people to be with you for the birth. (Note: Check with where you are delivering as to how many people can be with you).

Prayer: Jesus please lay the right person, or people, on my heart to have present at my child's birth. Prepare their hearts for me to ask them. Make them into the support I need them to be to help me through this experience. Make faith rise up within them to partner with me for the things I am believing for.

As my birthing partner/s I have chosen:

I feel they will be a good partner/s because:

These are the points I would like them to cover me in prayer for prior to delivery:

....

....

....

....

During labour I would like them to:

I will tell them I am in labour by:

I would like them to leave when or if:

Note: Write the above points down for your chosen birthing partner along with what you need them to do or bring using the page in the last section of this book.

I told my birthing partner/s that I wanted them at the birth and their reaction was:

....

....

Meet up with your birthing partner and share the journey you have had with God over the last few months. Go over your 'I am believing for' list with them and talk it through with them until they understand where you are coming from. Spend time praying together this week and over the next few weeks until delivery. Pray into your 'believing for' list. Pray for your baby, your body, the medical staff you will meet and everything else surrounding your birth. You will find that as you pray together that you become of one heart over this situation.

> *Matthew 18:19-20 Again I tell you, if two of you on earth agree (harmonise together, make a symphony together) about whatever [anything and everything] they may ask, it will come to pass and be done for them by My Father in heaven. For wherever two or three are gathered (drawn together as My followers) in (into) My name, there I AM in the midst of them. AMP*

Growth: This week, the average size is about 6.3 pounds (2859gm) now and 19.1 inches (48.6cm) in length. Your baby is officially full term now but can still benefit from extra days in the womb. A few weeks ago, your baby would move its eyes towards light. Now baby turns towards light outside the uterus. As the uterine wall stretches and thins, allowing more light to permeate, your baby develops daily activity cycles. Establish good patterns yourself encouraging your baby to do the same. So that after birth your baby's sleep cycle will be more convenient to your own cycle.

 *Week 38* - **Labour**

> *Psalm 23:1-6 The LORD is my shepherd, I lack nothing. He makes me lie down in green pastures, He leads me beside quiet waters, He refreshes my soul. He guides me along the right paths for His name's sake. Even though I walk through the darkest valley, I will fear no evil, for you are with me; your rod and your staff, they comfort me. You prepare a table before me in the presence of my enemies. You anoint my head with oil; my cup overflows. Surely your goodness and love will follow me all the days of my life, and I will dwell in the house of the LORD forever.*

Sometimes heading for labour can feel like a daunting path. Hopefully, over the last few months God has begun to renew your mind. Your relationship with Him has grown stronger and you are more reliant on Him. For some people the labour ward can feel like a den of enemies. Read the above verse again, He has made a table for you in the midst of your enemies! (I am not saying that hospital staff are really against you, please hear my heart, its just that what we feel isn't always accurate, especially when emotions and hormones are haywire!). But even in a situation where no one seems to understand where you are coming from, He walks with you. If everyone around you is pessimistic, if their cup is half empty, your cup is OVERFLOWING!

Labour for some people can be strenuous, tiring, hard work and sometimes even painful. God is the only one that can give us peace and rest in the midst of whatever situation we find ourselves in. He refreshes our soul and guides us through every moment.

When you think about your coming labour what do you feel?

....

....

....

....

....

Write here what you are expecting for your labour:

....
....
....
....
....

Regardless of the situation you find yourself in during labour what will you do?:

....
....
....
....
....

Circle below the top five emotional buzz words that you think you will have a sense of during your labour:

Calmness. Eagerness. Anxiety. Strength. Get it done. Peace. Joy. Faith. Reliance. Grace. Fear. Impatience. Confusion. Level-Headed. Capacity. Tears. Gentleness. Determination. Laughter. Fright. Tenacity. Believe. Endurance. Patience. Perseverance. Pressure. Pain. Delight. Health. Freedom. Certainty. Rest. Trust. Worry. Excitement. Overwhelmed. Capable. Endeavour. Autonomy. Seclusion. Team work. Mercy. Faithfulness. Speed. Humour. Understanding. Resolution. Devotion.

From circling various words can you see any areas where you are still fearful, or in your heart you're not in faith for heaven's standard?

....
....
....

Take some time with God and ask Him where these lowered standards and fears come from. Repent for where you fall short and ask God for His grace, faithfulness and mercy to see you through. Note here your thoughts on what you have just done:

....
....
....

Read the following exhortation from 1 Thessalonians 1:3-5, imagine this as being spoken over you. *"We remember before our God and Father your work produced by faith, your labour prompted by love, and your endurance inspired by hope in our Lord Jesus Christ. For we know, brothers and sisters loved by God, that He has chosen you, because our gospel came to you not simply with words but also with power, with the Holy Spirit and deep conviction."* Read these verses several times and note down how they make you feel:

....
....
....

Birth should be a partnership between you and God. You are creating life together. On our part it involves trusting that He is indeed faithful. *Psalm 71:6 From birth I have relied on you; you brought me forth from my mother's womb. I will ever praise you.* When you read this verse, how reliant do you feel on God?

When reading this Psalm how do you feel about birth?

....
....
....

Prayer: God I give you my labour. I choose to have peace about my finish line of labour, and to run the best I know how, with perseverance to the end. Jesus reveal to me the areas where I need to trust you more. I give you everything that I am still struggling with and receive your peace.

In your mind's eye ask God to take you somewhere peaceful. Write what you see and how this image makes you feel:

....
....
....
....
....

....
....
....
....

Spend a few moments and ask the Lord for any tools you can use during labour to keep you focused on Him:

....
....
....
....
....
....
....

Labour for me was a little like leading worship, it required the same mental capacity. When you are leading people into God's presence you are aware of what is going on in the room, how people are responding, those who are struggling, those who are not sure how to enter in. But the aim of worship-leading is to get lost in the glory yourself; to really meet with God yourself, to be one step ahead in revelation, so that you can pick the next song or know the flow of the worship. You are aware of what heaven is doing, you have engaged your mind to see Him and you look on Him with adoration, while still being aware of the people you are leading. In labour we need to be so aware of Heaven to get lost in the glory; know where God is; look upon Him; hear what He's revealing in that specific moment, whilst also being aware of our natural surroundings. In this way, no matter what your body is doing, although you are aware of it, the realm of the heavenlies is MORE real to you. If you can master this dual citizenship then anything is achievable.

> **Growth**: If your baby is the "average baby," they will weigh around 6.8 pounds (3083gm) and will be 19.6 inches (49.8cm) long. The breathing exercises cause amniotic fluid to get into baby's windpipe and coarse hiccups. These movements will be able to be seen by others.

 *Week 39* - **Tenacity**

Do you feel confident on the inside for what you have to do in labour?

Are you sure and certain?

Baby, these are my feelings now that you are almost here:

....

....

After your birth I expect I will feel:

....

....

This journey has been about relationship. You have been focusing on Him who is able. You have set the Lord before your sights. As you look to Him who is seated in a realm of glory you can be confident. *Psalm 16:8-9 I have set the LORD always before me; Because He is at my right hand I shall not be moved. Therefore my heart is glad, and my glory rejoices; My flesh also will rest in hope.* As you are confident in Him let rejoicing overtake you, be glad. You are seated right by the Lord and there is no better position. As you find this happy assurance you body is also at rest. The more at peace your body is, the easier labour will become.

How glad do you feel about the task set before you?

How unmoved in your convictions do you feel?

Have you found yourself rejoicing more often?

Read the following five verses about tenacity and faith. Evaluate to see if you share the same sentiments in your heart as you read:

Matthew 11:12 And from the days of John the Baptist until the present time, the kingdom of Heaven has endured violent assault, and violent men seize it by force [as a precious prize--a share in the heavenly kingdom is sought with most ardent zeal and intense exertion]. AMP

Hebrews 12:2-3 Fixing our eyes on Jesus, the pioneer and perfecter of faith. For the joy set before Him He endured the cross, scorning its shame, and sat down at the right hand of the throne of God. Consider Him who endured such opposition from sinners, so that you will not grow weary and lose heart.

Hebrews 10: 36 You need to persevere so that when you have done the will of God, you will receive what He has promised.

2 Timothy 1:7 For the Spirit God gave us does not make us timid, but gives us power, love and self-discipline.

Hebrews 11:1 Now faith is the assurance (the confirmation, the title deed) of the things [we] hope for, being the proof of things [we] do not see and the conviction of their reality [faith perceiving as real fact what is not revealed to the senses]. AMP

Prayer: God, increase my capacity for faith. Rise up in me inner zeal. God I see you, and know you. I know what you have promised. I know that your word is true. I know that you are good. I know that through your grace and faithfulness there is no reason I cannot attain the standard of Heaven that I am aiming for. Heaven is my home and its contents, my inheritance. I hear the great cloud of witnesses cheering me on. I can do this. You have won it for me and I get to walk in the goodness of that inheritance. You made the way for me, I follow you. I have no need to strive because I know that faith comes from a place of rest. I am sure and certain of what I can have and experience. I throw myself on your faithfulness. God bolster my faith so that I feel ready for what I have to do. I cast out all fear. I am not afraid. I am excited! I am ready. Bring it on!

After reading the prayer do you feel inspired and spurred on or fearful and doubtful you can do it?

Take what you feel back to God. Go back to His word and let it renew your mind. Ask Holy Spirit to reveal to you any areas of doubt and fear. Ask Him for boldness. Take the prayer above or write your own version on the following page and speak it over yourself whilst looking into a mirror, everyday, from now until labour. Say it until you mean it. Repeat it until you are whooping and shouting it with excitement!

I declare...

....
....
....
....
....
....
....
....
....
....
....
....
....

Growth: The baby continues laying on the fat stores that will help regulate body temperature after birth. In addition to normal fat, your baby is accumulating a special "brown" fat in the nape of its neck, between his shoulders and around organs. Brown fat cells are important for thermogenesis (generating heat) during the first weeks. Your infant's weight is around 7.25 pounds (3288gm) and length is 19.9 inches (50.7cm).

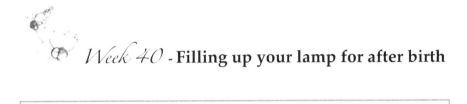

Week 40 - Filling up your lamp for after birth

> Matthew 25:1-3 *"At that time the kingdom of heaven will be like ten virgins who took their lamps and went out to meet the bridegroom. Five of them were foolish and five were wise. The foolish ones took their lamps but did not take any oil with them."*

We sometimes become so focused on the birth that having a baby in our arms seems like a distant reality. Do not forget to focus on the end goal, a child to raise! Do not become so focused on labour that it becomes like a mountain in front of you for which you spend all your energy and time pouring into the process of how to climb to the top that you forget to pack for the other side on the way down to your new normality of family life.

Find three things this week that you can do to fill up your lamp:

1:

2:

3:

I am preparing myself for my baby's arrival by:

Before the baby is born, practically I still need to:

At my last check up the midwife said:

What I love most about being pregnant is:

....

....

....

....

Around the largest part of my belly I measure:

I particularly love the following two verses for those with newborns.

> *Proverbs 11:25 A generous person will prosper; whoever refreshes others will be refreshed.*

> *Isaiah 40:11 He tends His flock like a shepherd: He gathers the lambs in His arms and carries them close to His heart; He gently leads those that have young.*

When you think of having your newborn in your arms how do you feel:

....

....

....

Are there any things that worry you:

....

....

....

Take these things to Jesus, He wants to lead you gently into the new process of parenting this child. Use the tools you have learnt throughout this journal to talk to God, give him your worry and ask Him for something in return. Continue to commune with God. Your life is a relationship and a supernatural lifestyle should be just that - a lifestyle. I found that pregnancy was a very intense spiritual learning curve for me, perhaps you have found the same thing. What I forgot and I want you to avoid, is that I was unprepared to carry through my new found supernatural drive and awareness of its reality, into my new role as a mother. Just like pregnancy, many negative mindsets surround parenting: the sleepless nights: risk of cot death: childhood disease: colic, terrible twos, troublesome threes, and teenagers! I found it relatively easy to stay on 'faith alert' during pregnancy because I knew that my due date was my end goal. The following eighteen years and beyond were a slightly more daunting timescale. Although the process of many years may not be as intense as the journey of pregnancy that you are about to complete, the principles you have learnt over the past nine months should carry through past labour. These principles should support your attitudes and decisions when you come in contact with negative views and mindsets in parenting and life.

Parenting 'supernaturally' should not be a daunting task. Once again God proves himself trustworthy of our reliance on Him. The Bible is full of promises for us, for all of our lives. As we take steps to live as the word instructs, as foreign as it can sometimes feel, the process of supernatural living becomes easier. Why? Because by living His word we begin to renew our minds.

Prayer: God, I am thankful that you will gently lead me when my baby arrives. I know that as I give to my newborn physically, and with all the love I have, you will lavish me with your refreshing love. I thank you that you will never leave me, but carry me through all that is ahead. Father, you are good and I rely on you to show me how to parent my child. I choose to spend time in your presence so that my lamp is filled with oil. Pour out on me Holy Spirit so that my cup is overflowing. God, I trust you. I place the life of my child in your very capable hands. Lead me and guide me gently in this next season. I love you, and I know you love me too, more than I know. Spirit I invite you to make me aware of God's love for me.

Spend some time processing through the following questions and prompt prayers:

Jesus, have I picked up any warped views on parenting from my own parents?

I choose to forgive my parents for not having the full understanding of your standard for parenting. I let them off.

Jesus, I hand to you these warped views and ask you to show me the more excellent way for parenting this child.

Jesus have I picked up any bad habits from my family that need to be broken over me to make me a better mother?

Jesus I hand you the learnt behaviours of (list all the things you feel have tried to come on you or your family, for example, anger, resentment etc.) Forgive me for partnering with them. Jesus I ask you to forgive my family line for partnering with and then teaching me these bad behaviours. I ask for your blood to cover me and my family now that I have recognised and repented from these sins. And I break every curse over me and my child that we will walk in the same behaviours. Jesus will you come and stand with me in the courts of the King. Because of you I know that my verdict is not guilty before Him. Show me that truth.

Reflection:

....
....
....
....
....
....
....
....
....
....
....
....
....
....
....

As we become parents it is important to see and be aware of where we have come from. Our fathers should be a representation of The Father to us. They often fall short of that calling and so we believe that Father God will treat us in the same way as our earthly father did. In the same way our mothers represent Holy Spirit to us. Holy Spirit in the Word is our comforter and teacher: these are typically roles of the mother on earth and if our mother wasn't a place of comfort to us, then we will pick up warped views of Holy Spirit. For example, if you had a controlling mother who always made you do things you didn't want to do, then chances are that you will believe that the Holy Spirit also will make you do things you don't want to do, (which could be falling over in the spirit or laugh or shake in His presence). As we strengthen our connections to the Godhead we see them for who they really are, not with our pre-conceived views made from the experience of our upbringing.

Father God, am I believing any lies about you?

As I give you this lie, what do you have for me in return?

Holy Spirit, am I believing any lies about you?

As I give you this lie, what truth do you have for me in return?

You can look at this exercise from the other direction. Can you think of things that God does, or things that people say about Him, either Father, Son or Holy Spirit, that don't sit well with you. For example, how do you feel about people calling Father God "Daddy"? If you have had a distant earthly Dad then chances are that you will not look at Father God as a 'Daddy' type.

Does it matter what you call Him? No not really but it's the underlying issue that I am addressing. In this example I would challenge you to pray a prayer of forgiveness over your Dad something like this: *"Dad, I choose to forgive you for being distant and aloof, for not showing your emotions to me and coming down to my level as a child. I forgive you for not playing with me and making me think that I was an irritation to you. I forgive you for being present but absent at the same time. I renounce the lie that you Father God would do the same. Father God will you show me the truth?"*

Write a brief list of things that don't sit well with you about God or what people say about Him, then see if you can make a connection between that and how your own parents raised you. You may find that you need to process some things through with Him:

....
....
....
....
....
....
....
....
....
....
....
....
....

Growth: 15% of your child's body is fat. Approximately 60 - 75 percent is water! The lungs will continue developing until birth. As your baby continues to grow; their hair and nails will grow longer as well. The average baby now weighs 7.6 pounds (3462gm) and is 20.2 inches (51.2cm) long.

✦

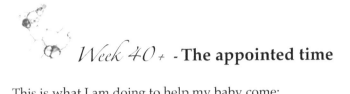 *Week 40+* - **The appointed time**

This is what I am doing to help my baby come:

This is how I feel about being pregnant past my due date:

....
....
....

This is what my midwife is saying:

....
....

This is what I want to happen:

....
....

This is what I am believing for:

> *Psalm 119:23-24 Though rulers sit together and slander me, your servant will meditate on your decrees. Your statutes are my delight; they are my counsellors.*

> *Philippians 1:6 Being confident of this, that He who began a good work in you will carry it on to completion until the day of Christ Jesus.*

Prayer: No matter what those around me are saying I know that I can still remain in a place of peace. I remember what you have said to me about my birth and I stand on that. I am confident that you will carry this through to the end and it will be good.

Remind yourself what God has said to you about your labour and beyond by writing a list here:

....

....

....

....

....

....

....

> *Ecclesiastes 3:1 There is a time for everything, and a season for every activity under the heavens.*

> *Habakkuk 2:3 For the revelation awaits an appointed time; it speaks of the end and will not prove false. Though it linger, wait for it; it will certainly come and will not delay.*

> *Psalm 126:5-6 Those who sow with tears will reap with songs of joy. Those who go out weeping, carrying seed to sow, will return with songs of joy, carrying sheaves with them.*

Prayer: God, I feel .... But I know that this day will surely come. I choose to remain calm. Saturated by your presence because it is there that I find rest and strength. From my strength comes joy. I choose to maintain an attitude of joy over frustration. I know that this baby will come at the appointed time and I will not strive to make it happen. I rest in your goodness. I will wait patiently. I will wait with faith. I know that at the end I will have a beautiful and healthy baby, which is my aim. I will not grow anxious.

This is what I am doing to maintain a place of peace and rest:

....

....

Get comfortable, put on some music, close your eyes and wait for His presence to engulf you. Let God's love flood every part of you as you rest in His presence. After you have rested in His presence, take time to listen to what God is saying to you. If you need to make a decision about being induced talk to God about it and find His peace on the matter. Write below what God communicates to you:

....
....
....
....
....
....
....
....
....

Because of what God told me I feel:

....
....
....

Declaration: Baby I can't wait to meet you. I love you. As your mother I am telling you that now is your time. Get into the correct position for birth. Body make yourself ready for labour. (Speak to your body and baby in specific areas that need moving). I proclaim that you will be born before...

Use this week to spend extra quality time with your husband and any other children you have. Write their feelings towards the new arrival here:

....
....
....
....
....
....
....

◆

Planning for Baby

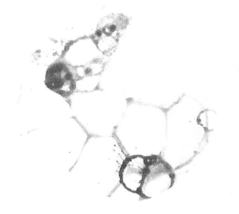

Questions to ask the midwife

When is my scan?

How much exercise should I be getting while I'm pregnant?

When can I go back to exercising after I deliver?

Do I need to be taking any vitamins?

What should I be eating or avoiding?

What can I take if I become ill?

When should I start to feel the baby move?

How often should I feel the baby move?

What changes can I expect my body to go through?

When should I go on maternity leave?

What maternity pay, if any, am I entitled to?

What does my body need to do to give birth?

What are my options for where to give birth?

Can I view these places?

Who can be with me when I give birth?

Who shall I call if I think I'm in labour?

What can I expect in labour?

When will my milk come in?

How long should I breast feed?

Contact numbers

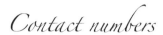

People to call when in labour, and useful numbers.

Name	Number	Occupation
		Midwife
		Doctors Surgery
		Birthing partner

Hospital Number:
Name of Midwife:
Doctors Name and address:

Gift list from my baby shower

Who organised your baby shower:

Where was it held:

Who was invited:

What did you enjoy most about it:

Gift	From

✦

Shopping checklist

Item needed	Store	Bought
Cot/travel cot		
Moses basket		
Bedding		
Blankets		
Baby chair		
High chair		
Plastic plates, spoons , etc.		
Bottles		
Sterilizer		
Dummy		
Muslins		
Bibs		
Toys		
Powdered milk		
Splash mat		
Car seat		
Pram		
Rain Cover		
Baby grows/vests		

Item needed	Store	Bought
Other baby clothes		
Scratch mitts		
Cotton wool		
Nappies		
Nappy bin		
Nappy sacks		
Baby bath or bath chair		
Baby toiletries		
Baby towels		
Room thermometer		
Play mat		
Cot mobile		
Breast pads		
Nipple cream		
Feeding bras		
Maternity pads		
Feeding shawl		
Baby carrier		
Wipes		
Vitamins		

Meal planner

Having a newborn in the house can be demanding work. Planning ahead can help a lot, especially in the first two weeks after delivery. Find a group of friends or people at church and ask them to help you. Use the schedule below and ask people to cook you meals for the first two weeks after giving birth. You can also ask them to help with the cleaning or taking older siblings to school. Try to make one extra portion per meal you cook for a few weeks leading up to birth and put that portion in the freezer, so all you need do is re heat what you have already made rather than cook a whole meal. Find slow cooker recipes and freeze all raw ingredients for each meal, pull out the bag the night before to defrost then place everything in the slow cook for a very easy meal. A week or so before your due date be sure to place an online order for groceries with your local store or milkman, this will ensure you never run out of the essentials in the first two weeks. Think about buying extra treats for older siblings to make them aware that you are thinking about them in this new and busy season. Little practical things like this can help you as you learn how to be a new family.

Day 1	Day 2	Day 3	Day 4	Day 5	Day 6	Day 7

Day 8	Day 9	Day 10	Day 11	Day 12	Day 13	Day 14

✦

Thoughts on parenting

Answer the questions below and reflect on different parenting styles. Read as many books as you can on parenting.

Question	Yes	No	Other	Reason
Will I breastfeed?				
Will I use a feeding routine?				
Will I use a dummy?				
Where will my baby nap?				
How long would I like the baby in my room?				
When would I like to start weaning?				
Will I use the baby led weaning technique?				
How old will my child be when I return to work?				
Will we have Godparents?				
Will I send my child to nursery?				
Will I use punishment?				
Will I use a naughty step?				

Question	Yes	No	Other	Reason
Where would I like to send my child to school?				
How old will my child be when I allow them to date?				

Talk to other parents to see different options and how they work. Have your partner read through the list too. Talk together about what kind of parents you want to be.

In what ways will your parenting style differ from your own upbringing?

What things will you do the same as your parents?

When your baby has arrived are you planning to dedicate them back to God? Dedication is a little different from a Christening. Christening teaches that the baby has 'made it' into the kingdom of God. I do believe that our babies are covered by our faith but there comes a time where they personally need to decide if they want to follow Christ. When you dedicate a baby you commit to bringing up your baby to know Christ the best you can, but you understand that at some point the child has to come to their own decision.

These are my thoughts on if we will dedicate the baby to God:

I would like the following people to be Godparents: (Godparents are like spiritual Mums and Dads, they will commit to uplift your child in prayer and input into their lives as and when they can).

This is why I have chosen them:

Siblings

If this is not your first child use this chapter to process how your new arrival will affect your family dynamic.

I told my child/ren I was pregnant at .... weeks

I have involved my older children in this pregnancy by:

They reacted by:

I gave them the following present:

I will introduce our new baby to their siblings by:

This is how I feel about having baby number:

I think it will change the dynamics of our family in the following way:

Prayer: God, I thank you for my expanding family. Give me the grace to parent a bigger family. Help me have wisdom to balance meeting the needs of all my children. Jesus I give you my family's dynamics, you know how many children I was going to have before the creation of the world. You know that this is going to work! Help this baby become immediately accepted by my other children and family members. I speak in, a bond of love between my children. I pray that they will be friends and live peacefully with each other.

What are your expectations of your older child/ren towards this new baby?

Do you have any fears as to how they will react?

Describe your relationships with your own siblings:

On a scale of 1-10, how close do you feel to your own siblings?

Imagine what a relationship score of ten out of ten would look like and write it below: (For example, being able to bear my heart with them.)

....
....
....
....

If you didn't score ten out of ten then spend some time forgiving your sibling/s for falling short of that perfect score. (For example, I forgive you... for not being safe for me to bear my heart to, for not taking the time to find out about me and to listen when I needed you to. I forgive you for putting yourself above me and for not loving me in the way that I needed you to.)

Jesus am I believing any lies about you that I learned from my siblings?

Jesus I hand you the lie that... and I ask you to show me your truth. Write what Jesus showed you:

....
....
....
....
....

We all want to be great parents but our past often dictates our future unless we deal with it. If we have taken offence at our siblings, however small, it will warp the way that we view our kids interacting together. Let's endeavour, through grace, to deal with our own baggage, so that we don't teach our children to hold onto the same views that we hold from an unhealthy perspective.

Encourage your older children write a letter or draw a picture about how they feel about their new sibling, write out the questions below on the back of their letter or drawing and have them fill in the blanks:

I am your big:
I think you are:
This is how old I am:
I would like to name you:

✦

Choosing a name

Throughout the Bible names are important. A name holds the person's character in its meaning. God often changed the names of people to make a point about their destiny. Choosing our children's names is no less important. God has given us the opportunity to partner with Him in creation, to name our child and speak over them their destiny and character. Words carry power. How much more then do the meanings of the names we choose, as we speak them like a daily declaration over our children, actually shape their very destiny. The bible is full of examples of people's names being changed to shape who they will become.

When choosing the names for our children my husband and I looked at what God had spoken to us about their characters and their callings. We looked at name books and did internet searches of names we liked. (You still have to like the name you call your child!) And we looked up their meanings. We also searched for the meaning and then picked the names we preferred.

Beth-Annily is our elder daughter. I have always liked the name Beth, but Beth just means 'house', so we looked to double barrel it with something that made it have meaning for our daughter. We found the name Annily, it's Ann and Emily put together. Ann means gracious and merciful and Emily means to strive, rival or excel. God had told us before we conceived, that our daughter would be strong in the spirit and strong in the flesh, so this seemed to fit perfectly. Beth-Annily = House of excellence.

Our son is called Reuben-River. Reuben means 'behold a son'. God had said to us that our son would walk in his true identity in Him; he would know who he is as a son of God. My husband always loved the name River and this also fit in because God had also talked to us about Reuben's position in the river of God like in the book of Ezekiel. So when you are choosing a name think about what God has said to you over your child as well as what you think sounds nice!

Write here what characteristics or callings God has told you your child will have:

....

....

Daddy's List:

Name	Boy / Girl	Meaning	Origin	Mummy's thoughts

Mummy's List:

Name	Boy / Girl	Meaning	Origin	Daddy's thoughts

What Funny conversations have you had about naming?

Have you considered names used before in your family line, if so why?

What names have reminded you of other people?

List four ridiculous names that you have seen whilst searching:
1:   2:
3:   4:

Faith not realised

- For those who are not first time mums or who have struggled through issues of faith in the past.

Have you had a previous bad experience of giving birth or any faith venture where you have had faith in God and it did not happen?

Are there things that you need to work through before you are able to stand in a place of faith again? You will need to wipe your slate of bad experiences clean before you are ready to go fully after and believe for this supernatural childbearing experience. I want you to be able to stand at the start line with no fear, self - doubt or doubt in God.

This is the previous bad experience I have had:
....
....
....

I was believing in God for:
....
....
....

I feel that I have been let down because:
....
....
....

Do you think God is faithful?

Do you believe that He is good?

Do you believe that He is good to you?
How do you explain not getting what you were believing for?
....
....
....

As you are reading this book and presumably wanting to go after the things of God again, you are more than on the right track. Even if this book was given to you, I believe it was God who placed it in your hands. He wants you whole and living in the standard of His word, regardless of what has gone before to disappoint you.

Are you ready to throw off disappointment?
If not, what do you feel holds you back?
....
....
....

Ask God to show you what disappointment looks like on you:
How does that make you feel:
....
....
....

Do you believe that God's word is true?
Do you believe that God doesn't value one person above another?
Do you believe that faith still works?
If you don't feel ready to be in faith for a pain-free birth again, which one thing can you be in faith for?
Spend some time with God and vent all the above answers to Him. He wants to hear your heart even if you are angry. God is not scared by your emotion, He wants to embrace you. Write a letter to God detailing all of your hurt, sorrow, lack of understanding, anger, injustice, pain, guilt, shame and resentment. Include the full depth of what you feel, be honest and frank, get it ALL out.

Dear God,

....
....
....
....
....
....
....
....
....
....

....
....
....
....
....
....
....
....
....
....
....
....
....
....
....
....
....
....
....
....
....
....
....
....
....
....
....
....

Speak out loud the following prayers and declarations. So that the entire supernatural realm can hear you. It helps you to hear yourself as well.

Prayer: God I forgive you. I feel that you have not come through for me. I could not see your faithfulness. But I release you from my judgements. I renounce the lie that I have believed, that you are not faithful, that you chose others above me, and that your word does not always work. God, show me the truth.

Wait on Him and He will reveal something to you. Write here what He showed you:

....
....
....

Prayer: I choose to embrace and to believe your word from now on. I see in your word that you are faithful and that you are no respecter of persons. I choose to forgive myself for not reaching the standard of heaven. I loose myself from my own judgement. I let myself off. I will no longer hold myself responsible for failure, I set myself free. Body, I forgive you for not functioning smoothly and I break every curse that I have laid upon you by my negative words. Body, I bless you for the work that you did do.

Jesus is there anyone else I need to forgive? (If people come to mind forgive them one by one, release them for the part they played and choose to bless them instead).

Hold your hands in front of you, visualise in the palms of your hands, all the pain your past experience brought you.

Prayer: Jesus come and take all my pain from me and heal all of my memories. (Wait for Him to come and take it). Jesus thank you for taking away all my pain. I will choose to live free from it. Holy Spirit, every time my mind takes me back to my past pain, remind me that Jesus took all my pain on the cross. Remind me that my slate is now clean, and today is a new day. Jesus I choose to throw off all disappointment. I trust you.

How do you feel now?

....
....
....
....
....
....

If you want to go after this again but don't feel completely ready, you can continue this exercise by asking the Godhead if you are believing any other lies about childbirth. Let Him reveal to you what they are. You can ask Him where you learnt that lie and then forgive all those you need to who had a hand in teaching you that wrong mindset. Once you have forgiven them, renounce the lie and ask God to show you the truth; accept the truth and make an exchange. This is a process to help you renew your mind and set your sights on things above. Pain can not simply be covered over: it needs to be healed.

To help you, when you read the list below, what feelings come to the surface?

- When I think about the medical staff involved I feel:

....
....
....

Jesus do I need to forgive any of them? (Forgiveness does not say that what they did was necessarily right or honouring of you).

- When I think about the way I conducted myself during this experience I:

....
....

- When I think about my birthing partner:

....
....

- When I think about God:

....
....

- When I think about books I have read of other people's experience of good labour, I feel:

....
....

Deal with each emotion as it comes up. Forgive those who you are harbouring resentment towards, including yourself and God. (You may not think you have any resentment, but if you cannot think of them or the circumstances without inwardly cringing or criticising then you probably do).

If after you have released people into forgiveness from the grip you have on them; after you have identified the lies you believe about childbirth and exchanged them with God's truth and you still cannot shift the memory of former trauma in labour; if every time you think about your previous labour you have a mental picture of that memory come to mind, ask Jesus to show you where He was in the room. Ask Him how He felt about you being in pain and suffering. Ask Him what He was doing to help you.

It's a good idea to process these bad experiences through with people. Women give birth everyday but if your experience was a traumatic one then you need to have the courage to ask for help from people you trust. Your memories need to be healed so that you are able to look at the same circumstance and not relive the former pain. Find someone you trust like your pastor. Show them this chapter and talk through what you have already done. You may just need a little help doing the last bit.

Finally, spend a moment with God and ask Him what your labour should have been like. Let Him take over your imagination and show you what He had planned for you. Write here what was revealed to you:

....
....
....
....
....
....
....
....
....
....
....
....
....
....
....
....
....
....
....
....
....
....
....
....
....
....
....
....
....

No more punishment

Sexual immorality

When you grow up in a Christian environment you can often be left with a lot of religious guilt when you do something wrong. Even if you did not grow up in church when you later become saved your former life can feel like a stain you carry around. All too often well-meaning Christians without realising can turn their noses down at those of us with a past pre or post being saved. Sin is often handled within the church with condemnation and shame instead of grace and love.

When Jesus died He did so once and for all. It was a complete forgiveness of sin and complete restoration of our relationship back to God. Sin is what separates us from God, but with forgiveness from Jesus we are now not separate from Him at all. The only thing that can break our relationship with Him is us distancing ourselves from Him either through choice or through sin. As soon as we repent we are straight back into His presence like nothing ever happened. There is a great misconception of who God is which makes us think even when we have repented and are once again able to enter His courts, He is still not happy with us or still punishes us for our behaviour even though we have said sorry.

We so often view God from warped paradigms without realising who He really is. Once again everything we do and think about Him must come from a place of intimacy that comes from spending time in His presence. If we don't know God as good then we can often view Him as the punisher; an angry God who hates sinners and who is out to teach us all a lesson. It is true that God hates sin but He loves us and as soon as we repent we are back to a relationship with Him without blemish. As far as the East is from the West that's how far He has taken our sin from us. (Psalm 103:12). God is not a punisher. We may still view Him through Old Testament lenses but He has moved on and so must we. ALL wrath was poured out on Jesus at Calvary, He has none left to punish you with. God is a God of choices. He lays a path of life before you but if you choose to walk a different road He is saddened, not angry, at you. He lovingly woos you back to His best for you. His kindness leads to repentance.

If in the past either before, outside or during your marriage, you have taken the path of sexual immorality, you have nothing to fear if you have repented. Forgiveness has been extended and His love covers a multitude of sins (1 Peter 4:8). They are covered over, dead and buried with Christ. You don't need to resurrect them in your mind, He no longer sees them because the blood has washed you completely clean. Nothing you have done in the past will dictate your future because He has extended His grace and mercy to you regardless of whether you slept with a thousand people or just crossed your toe over the line.

If what I am describing hits a nerve with you then process through with God the following questions and statements thinking of each sexual partner in turn:

Jesus, I choose to repent fully for any involvement I have had with sexual immorality. Today I plead your blood over my love life, over my marriage and over my children, born and unborn. I declare your grace is sufficient for me. I hand to you any lie I have been believing about your goodness. Jesus, show me any further areas where I am believing lies because of my sexual past. (Renounce each lie as it comes to you and ask Jesus to give you a truth to replace the lies. Write down the truths on a sheet of paper). Jesus, I thank you for your truth, I choose to apply it every time I start to think about the lies so that your truth can set me free. Jesus, show me how I look to you. Am I clean? Jesus, are you or Papa God angry with me because of my past sexual immorality? What do you think of me? Jesus I hand to you all guilt and shame and I place them at your cross and thank you for taking them from me, I choose to throw them off as you no longer stand in judgement over me. Jesus, which people do I still have soul ties with?
As any names come to you speak out - I break the soul tie between myself and... I give back to them what is theirs and take back from them that which is mine, washed in the blood of Jesus and made whole.
Jesus is the door to sexual sin open or closed in my life? If you see an opening ask Jesus if there is anyone you need to forgive in order for the door to be closed. Forgive those that come to mind. That could include a sexual partner, your parents, perhaps for not being more aware or yourself. Once you have forgiven then ask Jesus if the door is still open.

Children out of wedlock

His goodness will always draw us to repentance however it is inevitably easier for someone who has been sexually active to repent and move on if no fruit has come from those sexual encounters. For those of you who have had or are pregnant with a child and are not married it can be another matter. A church culture should be a safe haven, a place of unconditional love. Unmarried women with children should be welcomed with open caring arms, but often, what they feel instead is condemnation; forever smeared by their sexual immorality. The good news is that while the bride of Christ may be taking more time than one would hope to transform their mind into a heavenly way of thinking, Christ Himself is not only for you but fiercely loves you and protects you. By not having an abortion you have already won a great battle and have shown yourself to be strong. Churches should be applauding you but even if they are not He is and so are the angels and the great cloud of witnesses. What you now have is not a reason to be ashamed but a reason to rejoice, the life that you have or carry is as precious to God as the next person and He would extend to you and to you child, grace and mercy for every area of your lives. So brush off any guilt and shame and give it to the one who has covered you with His feathers (Psalm 91:3-5). Regardless of how your child came to be they have a glorious life ahead of them. You will not be punished with sleepless nights or a cranky teenager just because you have had them outside of wedlock, start to dream about what your child could become.

Pray through the following:

Jesus, I thank you that I am forgiven and fully restored to you. I throw off all guilt and shame, I will be proud to mother this child. I choose to forgive those that would scorn me and choose to revel in your grace and mercy. In my weakness you have proven yourself strong and I have a wonderful testimony. I choose to stand in the gap for my child and break any ungodly thing that would try and smear them regarding how they were conceived. I choose to forgive myself and my child's father and move on into what you have for me. I declare I will not lose out or be held back from my destiny.

Abortion

Many more women around us have had an abortion than we realise. It's time for the church to stop pointing fingers and help women come to terms with the emotions they are now facing. If you have had an abortion and are wanting to have another child I suggest that you take a blank sheet of paper and process through the questions I have laid out here. My aim is not to pile on condemnation. There were legitimate reasons you chose to have an abortion and you were free to make that choice. But if your decision has left you at any time in doubt, fear or shame then I would like to help where I can to free you from these burdens. I have never had an abortion personally but I do understand some of the feelings that lead to choosing one. When we thought that our first baby could be born with Down's Syndrome my mind took me to all kinds of places. I never entertained the thought of abortion per say, my view on it would not allow me. But I did go through a process of thinking that I would not be able to cope with a baby born with a disability and I concluded therefore that it would have been better not to have conceived or better for everyone if I miscarried. I was ashamed of my line of thinking but felt completely lost. It took me a while to grapple with my thoughts and to regain my peace. By pulling on the understanding that I can do all things through Christ, my peace returned. Once I had peace I was able to look at what the Bible says, to remember what God is like and what He won for me - then faith rose in me and I ended up seeing the breakthrough. But I still needed to forgive myself. I have found that this is the primary obstacle to overcome if you are to go onto have another baby. You need to release to God the unworthiness you may be feeling; to understand that nothing is unforgivable for God. As you let yourself off the hook it allows God into your heart to heal up the wounds of shame and guilt that fester. No matter what is in our past our future can be lived in spite of them.

When you think about your decision to have an abortion how do you feel?
What feelings have risen to the surface since the abortion?
How do you think, if at all, that the abortion will impact on the next pregnancy?
Are you struggling with feelings of undeserving?

Jesus I hand to you the negative feelings that I have. Jesus will you show me what you think of me?
Jesus if I ask you to take shame and guilt from me are you able?
Jesus is there anyone I need to forgive?
Do I need to let myself off the hook?
What do I need to do to be ready to forgive myself?
Jesus am I forgivable?
What lies am I believing because of this abortion?

What am I believing for this coming pregnancy as a result of the abortion? Jesus if I hand you this lie, what truth do you have for me in return?

You may find it useful to use these prompt questions to grapple with what is in your heart. Add your own questions and process your emotions through with God. I certainly advise that you find someone who can help you come to grips with the finished work of Jesus and therefore your worthiness. There are ministries and individuals who will help you reconnect with the Godhead. Talk with your pastor to find out who they would recommend. Throughout this journal I have used many tools taken from the Bethel Sozo ministry: their focus is on them facilitating you meeting with the Godhead rather than counselling you.
Their details can be found at the end of this book.

For Labour

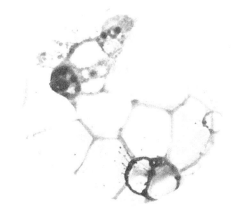

Hearing God's plan

Additional space from chapter two, Dream a little dream of me: Hearing God's plan and week seven of your journal.

....
....
....
....
....
....
....
....
....
....
....
....
....
....
....
....
....
....
....
....
....
....
....
....
....
....
....
....
....
....
....
....
....
....

✦

Scriptural blue prints - and what I am believing for

Scriptures	Brief Summery

I am believing for pregnancy that:

....
....
....
....
....
....
....
....

For the medical staff that I come in contact with to:

....
....
....
....

....
....

For labour:

....
....
....
....
....
....
....
....

For my baby:

....
....
....
....
....
....
....
....

For mothering a new born:

....
....
....
....
....
....
....
....

For any other area:

....
....
....
....
....

My birthing Plan...

I want to deliver at:

I want the following people present:

I want the lights to be:

I want to create an atmosphere of...   by...

I want to be in the following position during labour:

I want to be in the following position while delivering:

I want this food or drink available:

I want this equipment accessible:

These are the pain medications I am willing to consider if I need them:

I do not want:

I do/do not want skin to skin contact:

My baby is to be wrapped in:

This is who I want to cut the cord:

The person I want to hold my baby first is:

After delivery I want:

After delivery I don't want:

I am prepared for my baby to have the following medication:

I want my baby dressed in:

✦

My Labour play list...

Fill in the table below to create a playlist of songs to listen to during labour.

Track Name	Artist	Album	Order

Don't forget to transfer these to a CD or other device for the hospital.

Hospital bag checklist

A tick list of items needed for hospital.

Item	Packed
Baby's first outfit	
2 spare baby grows	
2 spare baby vests	
Nappies	
Cotton wool and small container for water	
Wipes	
Blanket	
Camera and charger or spare batteries	
Night cloths for me	
Change of clothes for me	
Lots of underwear	
Feeding bras	
Maternity pads	
Nipple cream	
Breast pads	
Toiletries	
Make up	
Hairbrush	
Towel	

Item	Packed
Purse, with change for phone if needed	
Contact number list	
Hospital notes	
MP3 player	
Book	
Bible	
Any scripture list or post-its you need	
Phone charger	
Pens	
Birthing ball	
Water birthing bath thermometer	
Change for parking or permits	

You will need to pack a bag even for a home birth just in case you need to go to hospital, but also it's helpful for your birthing partner that everything you need is in one place even if you stay at home.

For birthing partners

This is a brief description of what I am believing for:

....
....
....
....
....
....
....
....

Before labour I would like you to prepare by:

....
....
....
....
....

These are the prayer points I need you to cover me in:

....
....
....
....
....
....

This is my midwife's name:

This is my hospital number:

This is what I have been told to do when I go into labour:

....
....
....

When I go into labour make sure you:

....
....
....

Call the following people on these numbers when I go into labour:

....
....
....

Collect the following items when I go into labour:

....
....

During labour I would like to set the following atmosphere by:

....
....

During labour I would like you to:

....
....

I don't want you to do the following:

....
....

It is important to me that you:

....
....

I need you to help me with the following positions in labour:

....
....

This is the medication I am willing to consider if needed:

....
....

I am not willing to consider the following:

....
....

In my labour I want:

....

....

In my labour I do not want:

....

....

Once I have delivered I want you to:

....

....

Extra information:

....

....

....

....

....

....

....

....

....

....

This is why I have chosen you to be my birthing partner:

....

....

....

....

....

....

....

....

Make sure you photocopy this list prior to your delivery along with your birthing plan so that your birthing partner can familiarise themselves with it.

◆

Contraction Timings

Keep track of contractions below so that you can tell when you are ready to call the midwife. (Usually at around 3-5 minutes apart):

Time of contraction	Time between last contraction	Notes (change or stage or points to remember)

Daddy's time in labour!

It's Daddy. Mummy is in labour and I am:

....

I feel:

....

I can't wait to meet you because:

....

....

I am helping mummy by:

....

....

Mummy is:

....

....

This experience has made me feel differently about Mummy because:

....

....

When I think about becoming a daddy I feel:

....

....

Looking at you for the first time I feel:

....

This is what I would like your life to be like:

....

....

This is what I promise to do for you:

....

....

They're Here!

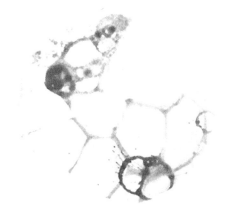

My labour...

A few days or a week after birth take some time to write up your labour story.

What would you do differently next time?

....
....
....

What would you do the same?

....
....
....

What items from your wish list did you see happen?

....
....
....

How was God involved in your labour and birth?

....
....
....

How was God faithful?

....
....
....

What was your midwife like?

....
....
....

Where did you end up giving birth?

....
....
....

Are you positive when retelling your story to other woman?

....

....

....

How will your testimony help others with their journey through childbearing?

....

....

....

How pleased are you with the way things turned out?

....

....

....

What are you not pleased about?

....

....

....

How does thinking of your birth make you feel?

....

....

....

If there are any areas that you were not happy with, spend some time now speaking these things out to Him. You need to process your experience through with Him. See if you have picked up any warped perceptions by asking if you are believing any lies based on your experience. You can refer to the 'Faith not realised' chapter for additional support.

This is my birth account:

....

....

....

....

....

....

First glance

This picture was taken at:
You were this old:
When I look at this picture I remember:
The very first time I saw you after birth I:

The day you were born

Date of birth:

Time of birth:

People present:

Baby's name:

Reason for name:

Agar score was:

At birth you looked:

Today's headlines:

Current top song:

Weather today:

When I went into labour Daddy was at:

When I went into labour I was at:

Your siblings went to:

-
-
-
-
-
-
-
-

✦

Footprints

Use paint or ink to print your baby's foot and hand print below:

Date of print:

Use this space to print your older children's hands here:

Date of print:

Siblings names and ages:

Questions to ask the health visitor

What are your thoughts on routine?

How many times a day should my baby be feeding?

How long should I let my baby sleep during the day?

How long should I let them sleep at night without a feed?

What is the best position to breast feed?

What kind of formula should I use?

Should I be giving my baby any vitamins?

How do I know when my baby is too hot?

Which way up should my baby sleep?

What benefits am I entitled to?

When are my baby's vaccinations?

Where can I get my baby weighed regularly?

Do I need to register my baby with my doctor?

When should I look to start weaning?

What ways can I get my older children involved?

-
-
-

Reflection

Looking back over the last nine months I feel:

....
....
....
....
....
....
....
....

This journal has helped me in the following ways:

....
....
....
....
....
....
....
....

My relationship with God has developed over my pregnancy in the following ways:

....
....
....
....
....
....
....
....

I would love to hear your testimonies, if you would like to share them with me then please send a copy of these answers to me via my website pragnancyinhispresence.com.

Endnotes

Title	Author	Source
1 - Pg 50 - The Five Love Languages For Children	Gary Chapman and Ross Campbell	Northfield Publishing May 1995
2 - Pg 60 - 'Meditate'	Hebrew word 'Hagah' Strongs reference: 1897	eliyah.com/lexicon
3 - Pg 60 - 'Meditate'	Hebrew word 'Siyach' Strongs reference: 7878	eliyah.com/lexicon
4 - Pg 68 - Food Matters - you are what you eat	Food Matters	Foodmatters.tv
5 - Pg 68 - Morning sickness - You can beat this	Karen Hurd	Karenhurd.com
6 - Pg 73 - Pollyanna:	Eleanor H Porter	Oxford Children's classics 2011
7 - Pg 88 - 'Heart'	Hebrew word in Luke 6:45 - 'kardia' Strongs reference: 2588 Hebrew word in Prov 23:7 - 'nephesh' Strongs reference: 5315	eliyah.com/lexicon
Biblical background and reference	Strongs online concordance	eliyah.com/lexicon

Title	Author	Source
Some of the tools in this journal are based on techniques developed by Bethel Sozo	Dawna De Silver & Teresa Leapshire	Bethel Church, Redding California. See bethelsozo.com for further details.
Biblical quotes throughout	The Message Bible New International Version New King James New Living Translation	biblegateway.com
Oxford American Dictionaries	Oxford University Press	All dictionary references were taken from the Apple dictionary widget
All growth box information taken from:	Pregnancy.org Care Confidential leaflets	Care